Deploraville

If ya don't like us, yer free ta leave!

Political Non-Fiction from Mac Balzac

Deploraville

Copyright © 2018 by Deplora Press

All rights reserved. No part of this book may be reproduced in any manner without the express written consent of the publisher, except in the case of brief excerpts in critical reviews or articles. All inquiries should be addressed to Deplora Press at swearengine66@yahoo.com.

#Deploraville
@mac_balzac/twitter.com
macbalzacpresents.blogspot.com

This book is dedicated first and foremost to my wife, whose consistent love, patience and wisdom knows no earthly bounds, and to my parents, brother, son, and my cats.

Table of Contents

Introduction 1

Ten Deplorable Commandments 3

President Trump's 2017 Fake News Awards 4

I. Playing The Game & Winning The Culture War 7

1. Donald J. Trump: Jazz Genius 8

2. Deplorable Rock Star to Sloppy Steve to Benedict Bannon 17

3. Thank You, Mike Cernovich 24

4. Apologize! 33

5. Assassins in The Park 35

6. Griffin-Gate 38

7. Pigskin Pigheadedness 41

8. Olbermann is F*cking Crazy 46

9. The Wolff In Sheep's Clothing 59

II. Deplorables Rising 67

10. Deplorable State of the Union 68

11. Trump is Who the Globalists Wanted is *Totally Wrong!* 87

12. Globalism Unmasked 96

13. The America First Party (A1P): Globalist-Free and Proud 103

14. Putin, Trump & Deplorables' Uncommon Common Sense 108

III. In Defense of The West........................... 115

15. Germany: Ground Zero for Globalist Defeat and Nationalist Revival .. 116

16. French Cheese Smells Bad but Tastes Good!................... 121

17. Dutch Deplorablization: Too Little Too Late?................. 126

18. Up Against The Wall.. 133

19. De-Golemizing Globalist Israel............................. 136

20. China-US Relations: Heightened Tensions Obscuring
    Golden Opportunity.. 142

21. Kim Jong-Un to Kim Win-Win................................. 149

IV. Know Thy Enemy, Know Thy Self....................... 153

22. #Syria: The Big White Lie that Succeeded Spectacularly 154

23. Pittsburgh not Paris....................................... 161

24. #SethRich 164

25. Pissed Off about #Parkland!................................ 167

26. Hey Deep State! Who *You* Gonna Call?...................... 173

27. Radical Islamic Terrorism: Explosive Distraction from
    the Moderate Threat 181

28. Head for the Turn Around................................... 188

29. Basic Bitch to Deplorable Patriot 195

Make America Great Again

America First

Build The Wall

Drain The Swamp

Lock Her Up!

Introduction

You could put half of Trump's supporters into the Basket of Deplorables. Right? The racist, sexist, homophobic, xenophobic, Islamophobic—you name it. And unfortunately, there are people like that. And he has lifted them up.

Hillary Clinton
2016 Presidential Campaign

In this book, the first in a series, I observe and analyze the politics, philosophy, culture, mindset and strategies specific to the brave men, women and children of the leaderless Deplorable Movement, its *de facto* head, President Donald J. Trump, and its many Deep State adversaries.

For much of my life, the idea of getting involved in politics seemed pointless. I simply took no interest. Later, when events like 9/11 forced me to start paying attention, what I began to see was so dark and troubling, I was really tempted to just let it be. But I'm the type of person who, once I understand something—and that can often take a long time—can't just stand by and do nothing. History is something one doesn't just observe but lives.

> ***Deploraville*** is about Deplorables, for Deplorables, by a Deplorable (and for anyone else who'd like to get to know us better).

I was determined to understand what Deep State and its anti-American, anti-Christian, anti-Nation-State, New World Order program really is, how it works and what its tactics and strategies are. I began to do more focused historical research and chip away at my fear of retribution.

I became more detached, viewed politics from a Big Picture perspective, and began seeing it more as a serious game than a life or death struggle.

This new perspective allowed me to probe Deep State for weaknesses and even challenge it in small ways without letting my emotions get in the way. Writing *Deploraville* represents a major step-up in my game, but it's just an opening salvo.

While Deplorables are indeed in the midst of a protracted war, to avoid falling into the trap of a purely Good vs Evil binary paradigm, tread lightly and keep your sense of humor intact. Winning's not much fun without it.

And so it begins...

Ten Deplorable Commandments

1. To defeat the Globalist Deep State Goliath, Deplorable Davids must be willing to bear at least one if not all of the following: arms, memes, energy, money, time, pens and ploughshares.

2. Any Deplorable worth his or her salt must clearly choose between the following: Anti-Globalism or Globalism, The State or Deep State, Freedom or Slavery, Truth or Lies, Beauty or Degradation, Creation or Destruction, Life or Death.

3. No Individual Freedom without preservation of National Sovereignty.

4. The Movement trumps "The Man."

5. CNN is CIA; CIA is CNN; MSNBC is MS13; MS13 is MSNBC.

6. The strength of a nation is derived less from its size and more from the impenetrability of its boundaries.

7. Mainstream media is to journalism as Pornhub is to lovemaking.

8. They're all Globalists until proven otherwise.

9. 911 was an inside job. Duh.

10. A nation without enemies is a nation without character.

The President's 2017 Fake News Awards

The establishment and their media enablers will control over this nation through means that are very well known. Anyone who challenges their control is deemed a sexist, a racist, a xenophobe and morally deformed.

Donald Trump
2016 Presidential Campaign

Mainstream media had its reputation tarnished claiming Hillary Clinton had the election in the bag. It then resorted to slander against its Alt media & Citizen Journalist enemies, smearing them as "Fake News." Little did they realize they would soon beg *us* to stop calling *them* Fake News.

> In an age when nobody trusts the media, taking them on makes you popular.
> Milo, *Dangerous* "Why The Media Hates Me"

On January 27th, 2018, President Trump announced the winners on Twitter:

"And the FAKE NEWS winners are..."

1. *The New York Times'* Paul Krugman claimed on the day of President Trump's historic, landslide victory that the economy would never recover.

2. *ABC News'* Brian Ross CHOKES and sends markets in a downward spiral with false report.

3. *CNN* FALSELY reported that candidate Donald Trump and his son Donald J. Trump, Jr. had access to hacked documents from *WikiLeaks*.

4. *TIME* FALSELY reported President Trump removed a bust of Martin Luther King, Jr. from the Oval Office.

5. *Washington Post* FALSELY reported the President's massive sold-out rally in Pensacola, Florida was empty. Dishonest reporter showed picture of empty arena HOURS before crowd started pouring in.

6. *CNN* FALSELY edited a video to make it appear President Trump defiantly overfed fish during a visit with the Japanese prime minister. Japanese PM actually led the way with the feeding.

7. *CNN* FALSELY reported about Anthony Scaramucci's meeting with a Russian, but retracted it due to a "significant breakdown in process."

8. *Newsweek* FALSELY reported that Polish First Lady Agata Kornhauser-Duda did not shake President Trump's hand.

9. *CNN* FALSELY reported that former FBI Director James Comey would dispute President Trump's claim that he was told he is not under investigation.

10. *The New York Times* FALSELY claimed on the front page that the Trump administration had hidden a climate report.

11. And last, but not least: "RUSSIA COLLUSION!" Russian collusion is perhaps the greatest hoax perpetrated on the American people. THERE IS NO COLLUSION!

C'mon in. Grab your covfefe. We've got a lot to talk about.

Scott Adams, *Coffee with Scott Adams*

I

Playing The Game

&

Winning The Culture War

1 Donald J. Trump: Jazz Genius

I pay close attention to tempo because I know that it's vital to keep the momentum going at all times.

Donald J. Trump
Trump 101: The Way to Success

The key to understanding President Trump, which most Fake News scribblers like Michael Wolff and even respectable chroniclers of this President seem to completely miss, is that at heart and in practice, Donald Trump is really a Jazz Man and our first Jazz President. In an unending daily stream, media provides the "Standards" and Trump synthesizes them all via his preferred instruments: Twitter, phones, speeches, negotiations, and conversation.

Most people don't understand Jazz. They hear it and they run away. People are frightened of what they don't understand. Not surprising then that Trump is and will always be a polarizing figure. But as Paul Newman once famously said, "A man with no enemies is a man with no character."

In order to improvise and swing in Jazz, it requires many, many years of practice and knowledge of the tunes. Only with that knowledge of the songs and their different melodies and harmonies can the Jazz musician not only effectively improvise, but make that improvisation appear so effortless. That's why many people are perplexed by the Trump brand of genius. It appears so effortless that if you blink, you might think it doesn't exist at all. Ummm...not quite.

Trump has been swinging to the media standards for years as a businessman, promoter and media personality.

As Candidate Trump and now President Trump, he well understands that he's not just playing Madison Square Garden or Radio City. He's playing The Statue of Liberty. Every. Single. Day. Morning, Noon and Night.

Trump's methodology and process have over the years remained largely unchanged. He channels the "music" he hears—fake news included—from as many media sources as possible, which includes Alternative media, Citizen Journalism and Social Media and then writes his own tunes. With complete awareness of his craft, Trump wakes up early and tweets what he's channeled from the day before. Throughout the day, he watches and gages how those Tweets play with the American public and the world as he goes about the Presidential business *du jour*: meetings, signings, speeches, hirings, firings, and whatnot.

> My style is based on trying to make whatever I do breathtakingly beautiful.
> Donald J. Trump
> *Trump 101: The Way to Success*

At night he consumes more news and reports – some classified and some not – and also works the phones. With near superhuman strength, energy and determination, he tirelessly pitches, promotes and sells the world's AAA-rated #1 brand: *America*.

Trump's mission and vision is powerful in its simplicity and singularity of purpose: *Make America Great Again* (MAGA). He's already very rich, so gaining more personal wealth at this point is not his main objective. He's 71 years old. He's got a great wife, great kids, and even great grandkids! (ask the Chinese if you don't believe it!).

So for the man who has everything, what's next? MAGA, MAGA, MAGA!

Making America prosperous again is his prosperity. The country's wealth is his wealth. Trump gets the Big Picture. He gets Persuasion. He gets Branding. He's been doing the Patriot gig for most of his adult life, but he's gone about it so humbly (yes, Donald Trump has a humble side) that no one noticed because he hid it in plain sight by masking it in brashness.

Much of the problem people have with Trump is akin to those who want their President to play the songs exactly the way they're written. They want Classical, but Trump isn't that kind of musician. His music is rebellious like rock and swings hard like the best jazz.

"Trump's not Presidential!" is the most frequent charge heard amongst his critics. I would agree that he's certainly not Presidential in the classic sense. A guy like former President Obama looked the part much better than Trump. Obama talked the talk, but did he walk the walk?

POTUS 44 never upset the applecart like POTUS 45. Obama's presidential decorum, at least in public, was impeccable. He played by the rules. He did what the Establishment expected of him. They handed him the sheet music and he dutifully played the score. No imagination necessary. Problem however was simple: Obama was not a patriot. He may have been many things to many people, but sadly, an American Patriot Barack Hussein Obama was not. Have you seen his Presidential Portrait?

Trump on the other hand, and even his fiercest critics can't really deny it, is a genuine, Real McCoy, dyed-in-the-wool, red, white and blue Patriot with a capital P.

But when you scratch the surface of Trump's patriotic exterior, it's delightful to discover there's more. Much more. Trump is an Improvisor *par excellence*. He's what *Dilbert* creator Scott Adams calls in his fabulous book, *Win Bigly* (you'll learn far more about the President from Adams than you ever will from Michael Wolff), a Master Persuader. He's got what Adams calls a winning "Talent Stack" (a wide array of talents that may not have any one talent as the best ever, but a total number of strong talents that's practically unmatched by anyone).

He's a risk-taker. He's his own man. He accepts that he's going to make some mistakes - sometimes big mistakes along the way - but he's confident that he'll not only be able to correct those errors but learn from them and evolve.

Trump is often criticized for not being much of a reader, and this may very well be true, but he's a voracious interpreter and synthesizer of all the many pieces of information he consumes each day. I get it, because in my own smaller-scale way, as a writer and internet-based Deplorable warrior troll, I go through a similar process. Every morning I wake up, check the news via Twitter and Drudge, which includes snippets of tweets, articles and video, and then collate and synthesize that info into my daily memes, quote tweets and original tweets. I go about my daily writing business which includes book research, book writing, book business, book and brand promotion.

I have household, pet and family obligations. I work out. I hang with the lovely and talented Mrs. B. We make and share dinner together. We watch some TV (usually *Infowars*). She goes to sleep, but I stay up a bit longer 'cause my work is just getting started.

In the wee hours I often Tweet more—sometimes retweeting what I determine to be my best and most important Tweets from earlier in the day. I often get inspired and write some more. Usually by this point in the evening, one cat is sleeping on my chest or lap, while the other is nestled up next to me and I'm starting to nod out.

That's my method. It swings. It evolves. It's fun.

Media Maestro that he is, Trump recognizes that he's driving the news cycle. That's his job. MAGA depends on it. And he's having a blast doing it.

Trump understands that in order to Swing and make great music, the raw material is by its nature chaotic. It's his job to channel and synthetize that chaos to make great music out of it. To MAGA.

Essential to the artist's craft is the careful doling out of what you wish to reveal versus what you wish to conceal. A caricaturist like Michael Wolff, as one can plainly see after reading his 300-page gossip column, *Fire and Fury*, only sees what he's been permitted to see. He's not privy to any of Trump's conversations, nor the many, many, many people Trump speaks to and what he speaks to them about.

As president, Trump has access to all the critical national intelligence. He knows exactly what Hillary's done. He knows exactly what McCain's done. He even knows exactly what Obama's done. He *knows*.

This is why the Deep State Establishment has been so desperate to overturn the Trump Presidency in any way possible. It wants to hold on to power no matter how high the price. Deep State doesn't care a whit if in the process they destroy the country. They understood all too well that a Trump presidency meant Trump would take power at their expense. There can only be one Band Leader.

Deep State held the reins of power for so long, they grew fat, corrupt, spoiled, and petulant. Funny how those are often precisely the charges Trump's enemies level at him! But that's who they are. Projection is a devastating mental disorder.

The big difference between President Trump and Deep State is that Deep State is cunning but not creative. It mimics but is incapable of improvisation. It fears, loathes and is envious of true creativity like Trump's. It longs for the immortality that will always remain beyond its grasp, but clutches to power so tightly it's incapable of ever being – let alone enjoying – the moment. It wishes to leech off and co-opt this creative Deplorable spirit; to own it, lock it away, pervert and deflate it, but ultimately it fails. It cannot be done for that is not its divine purpose.

Deep State's true purpose —of which it is *totally unaware*—is to push people like us out of our comfort zone. To ass-kick us (for a while...) into action that we might normally be too lazy and/or complacent to take: to be one with God. Our birthright.

A large segment of the population wants everything to be predictable. They want to hear their music played exactly the way they've been hearing it for years. In an uncertain, often dangerous world, there's comfort and security in that. Many are deathly afraid of taking risks in their lives. They want to be told what to do and how to do it. While that may be the Globalist way, is that really the American way? This country was built on the Pioneer Spirit: innovation, creativity, high energy, achievement, boldness, adventure, risk, and *fun!*

The Politically Correct, divisive, Cultural Marxist Identity Politics practiced by the Establishment is anti-American. It fosters cult-like, zombie behavior It runs counter to everything that once made this country great—values such as Free Speech, Christian Virtue, the Rule of Law, the right to defend ourselves against aggression, coherent nuclear families: all of which helped make us leaders among nations. But don't tell MSNBC's Joy Reid that. If you do, she'll accuse you of being stuck in the 1950s. Perhaps it's Joy who's stuck in the 1960s!

You don't necessarily have to understand Jazz—that uniquely American music—to love it. To feel it swing. The Mainstream media are a bunch of squares who it's our duty to troll. It's easy and it's fun. Just as I know it is for Trump, Fake News is, in its oppositional, deceitful state, a constant source of not only exasperation, but more importantly, inspiration.

Trump isn't perfect (perfection would be dreadfully boring). Only God is perfect. God finds the eternal so dull he incarnates in all of us on Earth to enjoy the full range of human (and all other creatures') experiences.

Trump, by necessity then, just like each and every one of us, is a flawed, flesh and blood human being, who no doubt has his moments of anger, pettiness, jealousy, envy, self-indulgence and every other sin you can think of. But as the Bible wisely tells us, "Let he who hath not sinned cast the first stone."

That said, by and large Trump's actions, and the fruits of those actions that fall from the tree, prove the man's heart is in the right place.

Politicians—lawyers typically—are reactive and predictable literalists. They need scripts. They need teleprompters. They're replaceable cogs in the Globalists' heartless, humorless machine. They're servants; not masters.

Trump is the opposite of a lawyer, and this is why the Establishment Wily Coyotes are beside themselves. It's why everything they do *vis a vis* Trump turns out wrong. No matter how detailed and thought-out their plots, schemes and coups may be, they all invariably end up working against them. Boomerangs each and every one.

The State of the Union address (SOTU) was special. Earlier that day I told my Twitter followers it was gonna be lit. And it was. Why? Trump cannot do anything but deliver. As Alex Jones, someone who unlike Michael Wolff actually speaks to the President, is fond of saying, "The man is OCD about delivering on his promises."

Former FBI Deputy Director Andrew McCabe is out. The shot-across-the-bow Nunes Memo has been released, and the "Horowitz Howitzer" (Inspector General Michael Horowitz's report) *aka* "The Horowitzer," is aimed and ready to fire at will upon enemy Globalist coup plotters' positions. What a time to be alive!

Never could have imagined that I, Mac Balzac, your humble Meme-Meister Mac, would have the honor and privilege at this critical moment to serve the nation by helping document, transcribe and synthesize this Second American Revolution.

We've come a long way baby, and we've only just begun.

Let's end this transmission on the President's signature refrain from the SOTU: "Americans are dreamers too."

The man even makes music out of *immigration*.

Jazz Genius.

2 Deplorable Rock Star to Sloppy Steve to Benedict Bannon

Steve Bannon has nothing to do with me or my Presidency. When he was fired, he not only lost his job, he lost his mind.

Donald Trump
Official Statement
January 3, 2018

Sloppy Steve sat on #TheWall
Sloppy Steve had a YUUUGE Fall
Neither all the Deplorables
Nor all POTUS' Men
Could put #SloppySteve back together again.

Mac Balzac
January 10, 2018

Sometimes you *can* judge a book by its cover. Steve Bannon not only *looks* sloppy, he *is* sloppy. But Bannon is a cautionary tale. Why?

1) Bannon tried to punk POTUS and failed.

Steve pretends to be at war with the media, which he calls the opposition party, yet he spent his time at the White House leaking false information to the media to make himself seem far more important than he was. It's the only thing he does well.

Donald Trump
Official Statement
January 3, 2018

2) Bannon punked a lot of us Deplorables (myself included) into thinking he was a gold standard-bearer of The Movement's nationalist ideology. He never was. *Infowars* reported that Bannon was a ringleader in organizing—and in cahoots with the Mainstream media (Michael Wolff included)—the 25th Amendment "Trump's Crazy" meme. These treasonous actions showed Bannon's true colors.

3) Although Bannon thought he could enlist *Fire and Fury* author Michael Wolff to delegitimize and possibly oust the President via the 25th Amendment, Wolff was the one who ended up punking Bannon by using his access to publish a book that only succeeded in bringing down Bannon and not the President. Benedict Bannon is literally a traitor.

4) Saruman Bannon punked himself by believing his own press. He truly thought that he was the *auteur* and architect of Trump, the Trump Presidency and the Deplorable Movement. Shlubby Steve figured he had the right stuff to be president. Now look at him. It's all blown up in his face. He's lost two jobs (at the White House and *Breitbart*) and his credibility. He's also been cut off from funding by the Mercer family. Only the long arm of Sauron (Soros) and his Globalist minions like Chinese fugitive billionaire Miles Kwok remain, and they are very eager to help.

Though the hype around Bannon was so ubiquitous that few could have predicted such an Icarus-like trajectory, if there's a silver lining to Machiavellian Michael Wolff's fictitious book, it's that it exposed former Deplorable darling Steve Bannon for the opportunistic egoist and traitor he truly is.

Ironically enough, much of this sordid story begins with Wolff's November 18, 2016 *Hollywood Reporter* article, "Ringside with Steve Bannon at Trump Tower as the President-Elect's Strategist Plots an Entirely New Political Movement," where Wolff largely steered clear of editorializing or showing his true Never Trump hand that he would later (despite his disingenuous denial of the fact) exhibit in his work of fiction, *Fire and Fury*. At a time when Bannon was being excoriated as a racist anti-Semite (likely a red herring) in many mainstream publications as well as on Capitol Hill, Wolff played matador to the Bannon bull, as he allowed the now-disgraced former White House Chief Strategist to effectively counter those claims:

I'm not a white nationalist, I'm a nationalist. I'm an economic nationalist. Bannon, article from Michael Wolff, *Hollywood Reporter,* November 18, 2016.

I don't know what Bannon and Wolff's relationship was prior to publication of this article, but I have little doubt that although Wolff was never known for his honest reporting, Bannon owed him. This "reach-around" relationship led to Wolff being given free rein to as he describes in interviews, "sit on the couch" and roam the halls of the White House hen house on a seek-and-destroy mission to gather bits and pieces of gossip wherever he could find them and stitch those dubious threads into a very tall tale.

While Wolff claims his book is not about Steve Bannon but merely what he observed and was told by others at the White House, without having gained Bannon's trust (and Bannon thinking he could use Wolff to help bring down Trump), there would have been no White House access and no book.

What boggles the mind is that Bannon failed to see the writing on the wall that Trump was very much not going down, and the publishing of the book needed to be halted at all costs. But perhaps by that time it was simply too late. Bannon had to know that he would soon be going down in flames. The die had been cast and the Rubicon crossed.

But if that's the case, that Benedict Bannon knew he was in trouble, why not get ahead of it with immediate disavowals and apologies? He chose not to do that. Once the story broke, it took Bannon days to apologize (which Trump rightfully rejected), and he never denied having made such statements from *Fire and Fury* as:

Even if you thought that this (the Natalia Veselnitskaya meeting at Trump Tower) was not treasonous, or unpatriotic, or bad shit, and I happen to think it's all of that, you should have called the FBI immediately.

Bannon piles on:
The chance that Don Jr did not walk these jumos up to father's office on the twenty-sixth floor is zero.

They're going to crack Don Junior like an egg on national TV.

If you're not an avid *Infowars* viewer like I am, allow me to share a few additional tidbits. At various times during Year One of the Trump Administration, there were rumblings from longtime Trump ally Roger Stone that an isolated Steve Bannon was not only failing to build his political base with his White House and D.C. peers, he was also leaking profusely to the Mainstream media. Deplorable stalwart Alex Jones also recently confessed to having been privy to similar rumors (and worse) about Bannon but hesitated to report them because he didn't want to get down into those gossip-mongering weeds, and probably figured it was just an inevitable result of the usual political infighting that occurs in Washington. It wasn't, and Jones now expresses regret for not having reported sooner what he'd been hearing about from multiple reliable sources on Bannon. Clearly Schlubby Steve was a bad actor and a cancer that needed to be immediately removed from the White House.

But what about Bannon's street cred as an Economic Nationalist? Surely this would be sorely missed. Nah.

As it turns out, the person most responsible for laying down the ideological planks of the Deplorable Movement is not Steve 1: Bannon, but the unobtrusively effective Steve 2: Stephen Miller. Miller, who Wolff said that Bannon dismissively labeled his "typist," just so happens to be the 32-year old Senior Policy Adviser who wrote both Candidate Trump's defining 2016 Republican National Committee (RNC) Convention Speech as well as the 2017 Inauguration Speech. Unlike Bannon, Miller possesses the wisdom to never claim to be an *auteur* and/or architect of Trump. Trump is his own man whose nationalist roots span decades.

As for Michael Wolff, I've got to give the man his props for having executed a very effective strategy for infiltrating a White House that if not in chaos, was certainly in flux. Possum Wolff played the cards he was given brilliantly if not at all honestly. But hey, let's not be under any illusions: this is *war*, and Wolff, like we now know Bannon to be, is the enemy. If we didn't realize it before, we know it now.

Wolff strikes me as a literary version of film director, Oliver Stone, a man who shares a similar fondness for historical fiction. In Stone's popular films *Nixon* and *JFK*, he engages in the deceitful, manipulative, politically motivated practice of never making clear to his audience exactly what's fact and what's fiction. Sound familiar, Wolff Man Mike?

Maggie Haberman of the failing *New York Times (NYT)* referred to Wolff's book in a tweet that it is "notionally accurate." Good to see *NYT* set such a high journalistic bar...All I can say is: enjoy the shekels and your 15 minutes, Michael. I hope that losing any shred of journalistic integrity you may have previously had was worth it.

For Bannon, it was a remarkable rise from former Goldman Sachs investment banker, Hollywood producer and *Breitbart* editor (he's no Andrew Breitbart) to helping Trump win the general election and having a position carved out for him in the White House as Chief Strategist. But Sloppy Steve, never known for a high standard of personal hygiene and appearance, in a brazen attempt to bring down the President, got sloppy with the details, flew too close to the sun and came crashing down with a thud.

It would be tempting to say, "Oh how the Mighty have fallen," but Bannon never really was mighty in the first place. Most of his notoriety was pure hype generated from OPM (Other People's Money), and now it's become clear that based on his actions, Bannon bought into that hype more than anyone. It's truly heartbreaking to have to be so hard on someone like Steve Bannon, a man who I and many others in The Movement – for a time—truly admired.

Will there ever be redemption for Bannon? If he continues to allow his ego free rein, I see him meandering down a very dark path and sinking into the swamp we thought he was there to drain. Sad.

If I could give Steve some advice, it would be this:

It's not too late to stay true to The Movement. Though it will likely take years – probably many years – to prove your loyalty and regain some semblance of credibility, start by cleaning yourself up. Eat better. Dress better. Go to the gym. Start your own media company instead of living in the shadow of Andrew Breitbart, a man who, unlike you, not only talked the talk but walked the walk. Be your own man.

The issue now is about Americans looking to not get fucked over. Bannon, article from Michael Wolff, *Hollywood Reporter,* November 18, 2016.

Prophetic words, Steve. We the People and the President refused to allow you to fuck us over with your ill-conceived, sloppy attempt at a *coup d'etat*.

Now please do us all a favor: be a mensch.

3 Thank You, Mike Cernovich

Aaaaaaand we're back. Mike Cernovich

There're few like Mike who I look to on a daily basis to provide inspiration, strength, wisdom as well as provide the highest standard of journalism to fight the Globalists. If not for Mike, I never would've started doing intermittent fasting, hitting the gym hard and attacking my writing not just as a hobby but as a patriotic blood sport.

Mike is a nonstop work in progress. In just a couple of years, he went from being a best-selling Mindset author to becoming one of the country's top political journalists with over 400,000 Twitter followers, and a family man with a beautiful wife and baby daughter. He's also an award-winning documentary filmmaker and hosts the best Deplorable parties. What's next? Congress? The Great American Novel? With Mike you simply never know.

> Quickest way to trigger a Liberal is to mention Mike Cernovich.
> Mac Balzac

Before all these accomplishments had taken place, Mike was (in his words) a "basic bitch" bodybuilder and skirt-chasing constitutional criminal defense lawyer. And before that, he was a poor, depressed, overweight, cornhusking, bullied kid from the sticks of Flyover country, IL.

While *Gorilla Mindset* and *MAGA Mindset* are both must-reads, even more valuable is simply reading Mike's tweets, watching his videos, and reading his articles. Mike lives what he espouses, and social media is the perfect platform for him to showcase who he is and what his ideas are.

As a White House correspondent, Mike was among the first to call out Antifa violence when he turned the cameras on the White House Press Corps, asking them repeatedly why they refused to disavow violence against Trump supporters from Antifa and the Left. Mike was first to break the Susan Rice unmasking scandal, a story that the Mainstream media remains desperate to suppress. Mike broke the John Conyers sexual harassment story that not only caused the longtime Michigan Congressman to resign but forced scrutiny into the even bigger story of the Congressional Slush Fund used to shield harassers and pedophiles from public scrutiny and prosecution.

Mike had been highly critical of former National Security Counsel (NSC) Director, General H.R. McMaster and his hawkish approach to foreign policy, globalist ideology and globalist personnel hires. Mike has also been at the forefront of those criticizing the failure of the Trump administration to keep and hire Trump loyalists. All indications are he has the President's ear. Donald Trump, Jr. is also an avid Cernovich Twitter follower.

In March 2017, *60 Minutes* thought they could get away with doing a hit piece on Cernovich, calling his ideas "nonsense" and strongly inferring that he's a propagator of Fake News, but Cernovich outflanked them. Using his own *Gorilla Mindset* techniques, Cernovich out-prepared and out-strategized *60 Minutes* by holding up a mirror to their Fake News reporting and interviewing *them. On their dime. In his crib.* It was a thing of beauty to behold. If the segment (with huge ratings) had been a fight, it was Cernovich who landed all the punches.

Although Cernovich would later assert that the segment was relatively fair, longtime *60 Minutes* host, Scott Pelley, who astonishingly had final cut of this debacle for Team Mainstream media (MSM), projected his own perfidiousness on to Cernovich, as he futilely attempted to frame him as a Fake News con man, but only succeeded in showing *60 Minutes* to be the real con artists.

MSM is a PR agency for Deep State. Its job is to promote the interests of Deep State by any means necessary. Truth is not only not a priority, it's antithetical to MSM's purpose, because the New World Order (NWO) agenda has never been a plan that could be fully disclosed to the public. MSM, working hand-in-hand with Deep State-paid politicians in Washington, must sell the public on the Deep State agenda without ever disclosing what that agenda really is. Covering up Deep State pedophilia and the Globalist-funded Leftist-Islamic alliance is fundamental to the MSM's PR mission.

The reason MSM is on a crusade against what it calls "Fake News" is because authentic independent journalists like Mike Cernovich are kicking MSM's ass up and down the media sidewalk. Rather than compete in the marketplace of ideas as proper journalists should do, and which is something a well-informed and well-researched Alpha like Cernovich is more than happy to do, MSM hides behind Deep State's skirts, making cowardly attempts to smear, discredit and label Cernovich and others like him as fake news. If you don't believe me, ask Alex Jones. Ask Matt Drudge.

MSM believes it has the ability to make its "fake news" claims stick, because according to former President

Obama's *Countering Foreign Propaganda and Disinformation Act of 2016*, this bipartisan piece-of-crap legislation not only shuts down the free speech of its media competitors, but also legalizes the spreading of fake news propaganda by the MSM itself! Amazing! Total *1984*! If ever there was legislation President Trump needs to overturn, this is it.

So, as we can now more clearly see, the agenda behind this *60 Minutes* fake news story is not the promotion of truth, but the censorship of free speech and the promotion of false and distorted narratives that threaten the Deep State. Like what? Well...

With so much focus on the Cernovich-Pelley exchanges, what seems to have been largely missed about this historic (yes, historic) interview even by many other citizen journalists, is that hiding in plain sight is the Pedophilia cover-up interview of Comet Ping Pong Pizza's James Alefantis. Now I'm not here to make any claims about Alefantis' guilt or innocence, but *60 Minutes* thought this piece on Fake News—with numbers showing this to be their highest rated report in some time—was the ideal soap box from which to both proclaim Mr. Alefantis' innocence and victimization while simultaneously demonizing his detractors.

Did *60 Minutes* succeed or fail in swaying Americans on Alefantis' innocence and victimhood? Answer: Fail! The Emperor has no clothes! MSM has no more credibility. Promotion by them, in the public's mind, is an implication of guilt! It's actually the worst kind of PR Alefantis could've received, even though Alefantis probably thinks it went great.

Let's keep two things in mind:

- MSM is the PR Agency of Deep State
- Pedophilia is the Achilles Heel of Deep State

The domestic and global Pedophilia/Human Trafficking ring is a massive problem. With more than 10,000 human trafficking arrests, President Trump and his administration are going after the problem with far more vigor than any previous American administration ever. Hillary and her crew: Bill, the Podestas, Abedin, Weiner along with a boatload of Establishment Republicans, Deep State Bureaucrats and major media figures are up to their eyeballs in pedophilia. Perhaps a *60 Minutes* Segment on Fake News would help...or would it?...

Deplorables are not dummies. We know what's going on, and we know that Comet Pizza and James Alefantis, whether they're limited hangouts, false flags, honeypots or whatnot, are part of a pedophilia nexus. If they weren't, there would simply be no need for Alefantis to appear on *60 Minutes*. What Alefantis did or did not do is unknown, but in the court of public opinion – and not whether he is actually guilty or innocent – his outline is forever etched in stone as a key figure in the larger pedophilia story. Sorry, James. Next time, if you don't want folks to get the wrong idea about you, try not leaving such damning and disgusting "artwork" on your Instagram account that might just give folks the wrong idea.

Unfortunately for Alefantis and *60 Minutes*, as with just about everything nowadays that Deep State, its paid politicians and PR agency MSM promotes, it backfires! MSM's effort to prop up Alefantis and by doing so hopefully put the Pedogate PR nightmare to bed has failed and failed miserably.

Cernovich's blows to Pelley and MSM actually were delivered less in terms of punches landed than a mirror upheld. When MSM's actions are held up to the Mirror of Truth, all the public can see is how fake, distorted and disingenuous they are.

MSM's *raison d'etre* is to provide cover for Deep State, and especially for its Achilles heel: pedophilia. What makes pedophilia the Achilles Heel? Having gone unprosecuted for so long, the pedophilia practice has grown so rampant and pervasive throughout the Deep State ranks that once the arrests start, they may not cease for a good long while, causing the whole Globalist house of cards to collapse.

Deep State needs to prevent this from happening at all costs, but it's losing ground as arrests have been made at an unprecedented rate, and especially since President Trump's recently issued Executive Order that specifies "Human Trafficking and Corruption" to be punishable by Military Tribunal. No more "Get Out of Jail Cards Free" from corrupt Liberal Judges in the pockets of the Globalist power structure.

Mike Cernovich and others like Alex Jones, Paul Joseph Watson, Mark Dice, Stefan Molyneux, Lionel, Vox Day, Scott Adams, Gavin McInnes *et al* represent an exciting new Trump-era breed of generous, humanity-promoting political journalists, analysts and commentators. And particularly in the case of Cernovich, he dutifully follows the principle of "giving to get."

Although he has slowed down a bit in recent months, nearly every day Cernovich produces for his followers a 30-45-minute video (or two) filled with up-to-date news and helpful information on the political topics *du jour* peppered with useful advice on how to lead more fulfilling lives. He's constantly writing new, enriching articles free of charge.

Mike provides useful and relevant advice—especially to men—about Mindset and Men's Health. He's written two great books: *Gorilla Mindset* and *MAGA Mindset*. He throws epic A-list (from a Deplorable perspective) parties like "DeploraBall" and "A Night for Freedom" and helps other Deplorables get together in meetups. He's a selfless, reliable friend and supporter of other Deplorable leaders in the Movement. He leverages minimal technology to maximum effect on multiple social and multimedia platforms as he reinforces his authentic self to his audience and encourages others to be similarly sincere about pursuing truth and authenticity in their own lives. Cernovich inspires.

According to Cernovich's law that states that when in doubt, bet on the more masculine man to win, Scott Pelley showed himself to be the Beta when he clearly did not do his homework on Alpha Mike Cernovich. If he had, he would've understood he was stepping into the ring of a heavyweight fight of which he was utterly unprepared to win. Hubris, arrogance and a sense of entitlement will do that, eh Scott?

Pelley and *60 Minutes* exist within an NWO echo chamber. They've gone so unchallenged—and as the Legacy Media so privileged for so long–they're simply unable to fathom what's happening in the real world. They've completely missed the shift in public perception. It's why they totally misjudged and misunderstood Trump and us

Deplorables, and why, as we saw with Rachel Maddow in her disastrous Trump Tax Returns segment, MSM doesn't seem to even recognize how out-of-touch it truly is.

Let's not forget: MSM has a job to do, which is to provide cover for the Deep State's NWO agenda. Ratings are important to MSM not so much because of profit, but because of reach. They need to reach the maximum number of viewers in order to spread their message—for which they now have legal cover under Obama's still-on-the-books *Countering Propaganda Act*—which in this case, as untouchable Kings of Fake News, is to smear others who expose their fake news and quash the anti-Globalist free speech that defeats them time and time again in the marketplace of ideas. Globalist bigwigs don't care a whit, whether it's an enemy like Mike Cernovich or their own operative like Scott Pelley who gets thrown under the bus along the way, as long as they feel they can reach the masses.

Pelley is a tool of Deep State. He's anything but an independent operator. Like most mired in swamp, Pelley has masters, and he dutifully follows orders when orders are given. Cernovich is the opposite. His work is all about freedom. He has no sponsors. The only product he sells on his platforms are his books, films and a line of quality, rigorously tested nutraceuticals. He answers to no one but himself and it shows.

Cernovich is as Cernovich does. He's gone from Nobody to Somebody through force of will. He screams authenticity and takes a Nietzshcean hammer to the world of Fake News and insincerity. That's why he has 400,000 Twitter followers, gets 100+ million Twitter impressions per week and is able to Live the Dream from the comfort of his own home. Everything that Cernovich is, Scott Pelley, *60 Minutes*, CBS, the MSM, the Globalists and their New World Order comrades are not.

Once upon a time, the Pre-Trump MSM could rather easily steamroll us into submission with their monopoly in the media marketplace. With an enemy now in control of the Executive branch and a growing number of Deplorable enemies in the field, MSM needs their monopoly more than ever in order to effectively perform their Deep State public relations duties.

On his way out the door, Obama and a corrupt legislature gave us an unwelcome parting gift in the form of an anti-Free Speech, pro-Propaganda bill in hopes of securing that monopoly in perpetuity. But lo and behold, the Globalist grip is slipping, and we Deplorables are here to pry their cold, dying fingers from the trigger. Not a job for the faint of heart, but Mike Cernovich continues grinding away to provide us keen insight on how to best get the job done.

<u>Postscript</u>: On April 6th, 2018, The <u>Miami Herald</u> joined Mike Cernovich's lawsuit (paid for out of his own pocket at considerable expense) to unseal records in convicted pedophile Jeffrey Epstein's "Lolita Express/Pedophile Island" case. According to subpoenaed plane logs, Bill Clinton has visited the island 26 times (without the usual presence of his security detail), while Hillary Clinton has visited six times. Numerous other prominent politicians, celebrities and businessmen have also flown on Epstein's plane and visited his privately owned island. Prior to the <u>Herald</u> having joined the suit, Cernovich was informed via reliable sources that he and his family's life were in danger if he continued speaking publicly about the case.

4 Apologize!

There are seasons in every country when noise and impudence pass current for worth; and in popular commotions especially, the clamors of interested and factious men are often mistaken for patriotism.

Alexander Hamilton
Founding Father of the United States

We don't care if you call us mean.
We don't care if you call us racists.
We don't care if you call us misogynists.
We laugh when you call us mentally ill for lifting weights.
We think it's hilarious that you think our attraction to women somehow merits scorn.

Mike Cernovich, MAGA Mindset

While Lady Gaga's Super Bowl (Patriots vs Falcons) halftime performance garnered much of the week's hype in the press, the pregame singing of "America the Beautiful" by the three actresses who played The Schuyler Sisters (Phillipa Soo, Renee Elise Goldsberry and Jasmine Cephas) in the Broadway musical, *Hamilton*, flew under the radar. It shouldn't have.

If you recall, on November 18th, 2016—nine days after Donald Trump was elected—at the conclusion of the performance, the actor playing Vice President Aaron Burr (Brandon Victor Dixon) addressed then Vice President-elect Mike Pence from the stage, saying:

We hope you will hear us out. We, sir—we—are the diverse America who are alarmed and anxious that your new administration will not protect us, our planet, our children, our parents, or defend us and uphold our inalienable rights. We truly hope that this show has inspired you to uphold our American values and to work on behalf of all of us.

While our classy and respectful Vice President stood stoically by and listened to this inappropriate, premeditated claptrap (a blatantly pre-planned effort led by the show's creator Lin-Manuel Miranda), President-elect Trump fumed, as he released two scathing tweets the following morning:

Our wonderful future V.P. Mike Pence was harassed last night at the theater by the cast of Hamilton, cameras blazing. This should not happen!

The Theater must always be a safe and special place. The cast of Hamilton was very rude last night to a very good man, Mike Pence. Apologize!

While Dixon, and his cohorts could have expressed contrition, they chose instead – as the Left often does to their own detriment—to double down when the actor defiantly tweeted back:

Conversation is not harassment, sir.

How disingenuous! In a crowded theater, when you have an actor speaking down to the audience from the stage, that's no conversation; it's a lecture!

I agree with the President. *Apologize!*

5   Assassins in The Park

The recent turn of events give rise to the observation that the defense of President Trump is the defense of America.

Rich Higgins
POTUS and *Political Warfare*

It's taken getting a true Nationalist into office in President Trump for us to notice just how tightly the decades-long Globalist grip on the Arts has been. Art under Globalist cultural Marxist control is absolutely a propaganda tool used to reinforce the anti-human, anti-family, anti-Christian, anti-national inverted values of the New World Order that keeps a docile, brainwashed population from realizing that they're being conned into serving as useful idiots and knaves of the ruling Elite.

> "Stop Leftist Violence!" Laura Loomer, from the stage at Shakespeare in the Park production of *Julius Caesar*

I'm speaking specifically of the audience that gets whipped up into frenzy at the sight of the President's assassination (it's the only reason for them to endure the entire subpar execution of the Shakespeare classic). It's time for Deplorable patriots to take The Arts back from the Globalists!

> "Goebbels would be proud!" Jack Posobiec from his seat at Shakespeare in the Park production of *Julius Caesar*

Former *Project Veritas* and *Rebel Media* reporter Laura Loomer's courageous act of taking the stage during the Central Park presentation of *Julius Caesar* and decrying leftist violence is the opening salvo. Loomer was arrested and charged for a completely non-violent act, while rampant Antifa violence across the country not only goes completely unnoticed and unreported by MSM, it also goes largely unpunished by law enforcement and the legal system. Talk about a double standard!

Jack Posobiec (rhymes with "heroic"), during that same performance, disrupted the action from his seat, repeatedly shouting "Goebbels would be proud!"

Jack, in a subsequent video, proceeded to describe to viewers how for the first time in his life he fully grasped the meaning of the expression "my blood ran cold," as moments earlier he witnessed the audience's cathartic, near-orgasmic blood lust prompted by the Trump/Caesar assassination scene. Indeed, Hitler's propagandist Joseph Goebbels surely would have been proud. No doubt Stalin and Mao—two of the most prolific mass murderers in history from the totalitarian Left – no doubt would also have been proud.

Unlike violent Antifa activists, we Deplorables will win this culture war non-violently with memes, intelligence and love—love for each other, love of country, love of God and even love for our twisted and confused enemies. Forgive them Father for they know not what they do. Violence should only be employed for reasons of self-defense.

The Globalists have it all wrong. Caesar is not Trump. Caesar is the Globalist power structure that not only desperately seeks to maintain its dominance over every aspect of our waking life but is especially prevalent over the The Arts. Isn't it high time we created our own

Deplorable theater, our own Deplorable late night talk shows, our own Deplorable *Saturday Night Live,* our own Deplorable films, and our own Deplorable books?

<u>Post-Script</u>: Trump-supporting Roseanne Barr and her mega-hit ABC show, <u>Roseanne</u> dominated the ratings with 18.2 million viewers. Thanks to <u>Roseanne's</u> smashing success<u>.</u> Deplorables no longer need to sit at the back of the Hollywood bus.

6 Griffin-Gate

If you feel yourself getting angry, immediately walk away. Go somewhere and cool down. When you are completely composed, discuss the situation with someone who can give you objective advice.
Donald Trump
Trump 101: The Way to Success

Kathy Griffin's "Trump Beheading" video underscored the Globalists' barely concealed blood-lust for violence against their political enemies and glorified the barbaric ISIS practice of beheading. Griffin would later double down in a subsequent videotaped "apology" and press conference by virtue signaling to the Left as she blamed all her woes on "Old White Men," which is ironic since these same "Old White Men" are responsible for helping Griffin become one of the highest paid comedians – male or female – in the world!

Amidst fake tears at this circus-like Hollywood press conference, Griffin proceeded to blame Donald Trump ("He broke me!") for her pain and suffering, which only made her even more of a laughingstock. In her pathetic presser, Griffin came across as a dumb, disingenuous, unbalanced, insecure, sadomasochistic (the beheading video was sadistic, while the press conference was masochistic) attention-whore.

While major *CNN* advertisers like ADT were quick to withdraw their ads from *CNN*, and venues where Griffin was booked to perform began cancelling her shows, it took the Counterfeit News Network *CNN* nearly a full 24 hours to fire Griffin from its upcoming New Year's Eve show. Waiting as long as they did implies tacit support for Griffin's reprehensible actions and further tarnishes the reputation of this Very Fake News outlet.

Project Veritas and the *CNN* Meme Wars would later provide the kill shot to *CNN*. With such questionable judgment, tacit and at times overt support for political violence, *CNN* – already dead but existing in full-on Zombie Apocalypse mode—is seeing its already failing brand (with a meager 6% approval rating according to a major poll) fall even further in terms of credibility.

When Chelsea Clinton and the Church of Satan—that's right, the friggin' *Church of Satan*—disavow Kathy Griffin before *CNN* does, it speaks volumes. Those who have come out to the media in support of Griffin include Jim Carrey, Alec Baldwin, Jerry Seinfeld and Senator/Comic Al Franken. They should all be ashamed of themselves.

Clearly Griffin was attempting to revive her moribund career by means of a highly calculated publicity stunt that although it did make headlines, was at the cost of inadvertently making herself universally reviled figure. Not exactly a good look and certainly not what she was going for. Career suicide?

One would like to think so, but this is probably just wishful thinking. Those on the Left, in Hollywood and among Deep State circles who support terrorism, political violence and pedophilia, and who can scarcely contain their unabashed hatred and jealousy of Donald Trump, no doubt furtively admire Griffin for what they did not have the (reckless) courage to do themselves and will therefore do what they can to help her.

Be that as it may, with the Griffin video, the "Kill Trump" meme has reached a tipping point with the American Public. Desperate wailing for assassination, even in the form of "comedy," is indicative of Globalist panic. They've thrown everything they've got at Trump and not only has nothing stuck; it's backfiring. Big time. Moderates on the Left and Right are recognizing that it's Trump who actually occupies the Center, and so they are more willing than ever to support him and other like-minded candidates.

Quoting Hammurabi, "make the punishment fit the crime." While Kathy Griffin should apologize personally to young Barron Trump (who was understandably shaken after seeing the viral video), the entire Trump family, and the nation, I propose as penance that she be made to clean public toilets for no less than one year beginning with the one at the White House Press Room—a facility which White House Press Correspondent Mike Cernovich has pointed out as being particularly disgusting.

Washed-up Kathy Griffin likely feels no sympathy for the Trumps and is only sorry that she ended up cutting off her own head. But it's really not such a bad thing. The more vile the act from Lunatic Liberals like Griffin, the better the President looks in contrast, and the easier it'll be to not only ram through his agenda, but also to get him re-elected in 2020 and 2024.

Thanks, Kathy.

7   Pigskin Pigheadedness

Wouldn't you love to see any one of these NFL owners, when somebody disrespects our flag, to say, "Get that son of a bitch off the field right now, Out. He's fired. He's fired!"

Donald Trump
September 22, 2016, Alabama Rally

Before getting into the politics, I'd like to make a relatively quick case for why Colin Kaepernick, a spoiled, virtue signaling Far-Leftist, and Tim Tebow, a respectful, humble Christian patriot are out of the league—and it has little to nothing to do with politics, and nearly everything to do with their similar football skillsets. At one time, not long ago, I was studying to be a football scout, so for those of you who are not really into sports, please forgive my brief diversion into football wonkiness, which I assure you will pay off in the end.

Both players. Kap and Tebow, happen to be athletic, running QBs who tend to struggle with accuracy from the pocket, but certainly would make a formidable duo for any team that was committed to running a Wildcat/Read Option-type offense. Unfortunately for both former players, this type of offensive strategy, while common at the collegiate level, tends to be frowned upon in the pros, where rules favor pocket passers and the risk of injury to franchise QBs is reduced. So, contrary to popular belief, it's this, and not their politics, that is the primary reason neither is currently employed by an NFL team.

Running QBs require a total offensive commitment that few teams are willing to make. Tebow and Kap are either starters or backups on Wildcat offenses, but they are neither on pocket-passing teams. It's simply not practical. For pocket passing teams, there needs to be a whole different set of plays for the backup QB, which also requires a different supporting cast to exploit that style of offense. NFL teams want backups who can throw from the pocket, don't cost them an arm and a leg, and don't throw shade (intentionally or not) upon their Franchise QBs. For all of these reasons, both Kap and Tebow are poor fits.

Personally, I like smash-mouth football, and I enjoy watching players like Kap and Tebow play when the offense is designed for them. They've both shown they can be successful when given that support. And now that NFL defenses have shifted to employing smaller, faster players who are more adept in pass coverage than tackling, it's a great time to go contrarian with running QBs like Kap and Tebow. In an ideal world, and from a pure football perspective, I think the two would make for ideal teammates. Meanwhile, thanks in part to Kaepernick and a lot of pigheaded hubris, the NFL, once the apple of the sports world eye, finds itself in perilously deep waters.

NFL Players, who for the most part know little about history or politics, continue making misguided protests about race in an inappropriate forum—a private league where owners have every right to, *"yank the sons of bitches off the field and fire them,"* but consistently fail to do so.

Though Trump's language may be salty, the fact remains that he has the moral high ground (America trumps the NFL) and is 100% correct. Despite outcries from the usual suspects like Maxine Waters and the corporate Mainstream media, Trump's position has absolutely nothing to do with race and everything to do with patriotism.

I don't blame the players. I blame the owners and the league. The players are disrespecting the nation, the anthem and the flag, but not because they're malicious. They're mainly immature, narcissistic, ill-informed child-athletes who don't know better. League Owners and Commisar Goodell do know better and seem to care more about virtue signaling to the Left that they're politically correct than standing up for the integrity of a game that is supported by a majority of fans who know that the nation is bigger—much bigger—than the NFL. Without America and the values it stands for, there is no NFL. America is the bigger brand. *The* biggest in the world.

While President Trump smartly wraps himself in the flag, he's successfully trolling the NFL (and NBA and ESPN) because he knows that most football fans are patriotic. They understand that the owners, the league and the players, by blatantly disrespecting the anthem and the flag, cannot help but look unpatriotic. Trump therefore looks good and the NFL looks bad. This is low-hanging Culture War fruit for the President that's much easier to pluck than trying to get bills passed by obstructionist Democrats and cucked GOP Establishment Republicans (GOPe).

Fans understand that not only are the protests wrongheaded, but the league and owners are too cowardly to take appropriate action. Meanwhile, the mainstream corporate media once again prove themselves dishonest by only covering one side of the story, as they completely ignore the "America First" fan perspective.

Deplorables see right through this naked hypocrisy and unbalanced fake media coverage.

Trump's opponents really aren't very bright. Scott Adams makes a great observation when he points out how poor and laughable the optics are when you *kneel* for something you *stand* against! While on one level it makes sense to kneel in protest against the anthem for which you are supposed to stand out of honor and respect for the nation, the act of kneeling is always viewed as an act of submission. So essentially, on a visual and symbolic level, the players and in some cases owners, are actually submitting to President Trump! Adams would no doubt rightly say, "That's poor persuasion!"

Adams even went as far as to predict that teams who knelt less over the course of the 2017 season would win more games than teams who knelt more, and this proved true. In fact, the two teams who knelt the least, the Patriots and the Eagles, played each other in the Super Bowl!

If Kap had been appropriately punished for the previous season's antics—preferably by the 49ers but also by the league—the NFL could've nipped this in the bud. That didn't happen, and now, by quadrupling down, the NFL has inflicted permanent damage upon its brand. But rather than begin to correct the problem, the NFL and its team owners gave the middle finger to their fans and the country. POTUS laid a trap for them and they fell for it hook, line and sinker.

As narcissistic, ignorant, inappropriate and wrongheaded as their actions may be, when kids are spoiled, blame the parents, who in this case are the league and the owners.

Having been raised according to cultural Marxist values and focused on elite level performance in their sport, most of these players are young men who've yet to awaken to political realities. We were all young once, so I really can't come down too hard on them. For a large portion of the country, which includes Academia, Hollywood, the Media and the Washington Establishment, it's trendy to bash Trump, so why should we expect NFL players to behave any different? The owners and the league, however, are another story. They erroneously thought they'd go ahead and show America that the NFL was bigger than the nation. Disrespecting the anthem and the flag is about as popular with fans as excessively celebrating a touchdown after being down 52-0 That just shows you're out of touch with reality, and it's never appropriate.

Failing to understand that it's America First and not the NFL is a lesson that a pigheaded league, its owners and players seem to wanna learn the hard way.

Football is a great game. Keep politics out of it. It kills the brand and spoils the fun.

8 Olbermann is F*cking Crazy

I guess the painkillers wipe out your memory along with your ethics.
                            Keith Olbermann

WARNING: If you like Keith Olbermann, you may not want to read this chapter. Anybody, anybody? Ok then...you're all still here...let's get started.

There's a part of me that says, "Why so hard on Olbermann? He never did anything to you. He found a niche called Trump bashing and he's exploiting it to feed his family (does Olbermann even have a family?). He's an actor. Am I being...*unkind?*"

Nah. Olbermann deserves it, and I'm probably being way too nice. If you have the arrogance, hubris, bravado, and *chutzpah* to write an unabashedly nasty book called *Trump is F*cking Crazy*, it would be crazy not to expect blowback.

Here are my Top 15 shoot-from-the-hip Keith Olbermann impressions I got from reading his morbidly entertaining shipwreck of a book:

1. Olbermann is to Losing as Trump is to Winning.

2. Olbermann wraps himself in the flag in order to wipe his snotty, America-thumbing nose with it.

3. Olbermann makes career suicide a national sport.

4. Hillary is to Penis Envy what Olbermann is to *Trumpis* Envy

5. It's a shame Olbermann only has two feet to stick in his mouth.

6. For Olbermann, the good news is he has seven more years of Trump material to share with the public. The bad news is, he won't be able to type his way out of the strait jacket.

7. The reason Olbermann's book is so hilarious is because he's not trying to be funny.

8. Trump is to Mr. Krabs as Olbermann is to Plankton.

9. The beauty of Olbermann and his book isn't just that he's wrong about Trump, he's *spectacularly* wrong about Trump.

10. Trump is crazy like a fox; Olbermann is just plain crazy.

11. Olbermann is the guy in the theater who dies from fire after setting the fire that he yelled fire about.

12. There's a clinical name for Olbermann's unique form of self-loathing. It's called Trump Derangement Syndrome (TDS) and it's highly contagious on the Left.

13. Olbermann is the wolf who tells the boy to cry wolf, eats the boy and then gets pitchforked by villagers.

14. Olbermann needs to get laid.

15. *Trump is F*cking Crazy* is a Posedion Adventure that miraculously only produces one casualty: Keith Olbermann.

A bit of back story on Olbermann:

In 2001, when asked about Olbermann, Fox's Rupert Murdoch said, "I fired him . . . He's crazy." (*Wikipedia*)

But Trump is F*cking Crazy.

Olbermann became frustrated when Countdown with Keith Olbermann *ate its own tail over the Monica Lewinsky scandal. In 1998, he stated that his work at MSNBC would "I'm ashamed of my work. It makes me depressed. It makes me want to cry. (Wikipedia)*

But it's Trump who's psychologically unstable.

Former Los Angeles Times television critic Howard Rosenberg*: Keith Olbermann's Countdown is more or less an echo chamber in which Olbermann and like-minded bobbleheads nod at each other. (Wikipedia)*

But it's Trump Supporters who are out of touch and operating within an echo chamber.

During the 2008 US presidential election, Olbermann co-anchored MSNBC's coverage with Chris Matthews until September, 2008, when they were replaced by David Gregory after complaints from outside and inside NBC that they were making partisan statements. This apparent conflict of interest had been an issue as early as May 2007, when Giuliani campaign officials complained about his serving as both host and commentator. (Wikipedia)

But it's Trump who's plagued by conflicts of interest.

After one year, Olbermann was fired from Current TV on March 30, 2012. In a statement from Current TV:

Current was founded on the values of respect, openness, collegiality, and loyalty to our viewers. Unfortunately, these values are no longer reflected in our relationship with Keith Olbermann and we have ended it.
But it's Trump who must be removed from office.

In August 1980, Olbermann suffered a head injury while leaping onto a New York City Subway train. This head injury permanently upset his equilibrium, resulting in his avoidance of driving. (Wikipedia)
But Trump is F*cking Crazy.

Olbermann believes that if he screams "Trump's F*cking Crazy" often enough it'll make it so. No, it only means *Olbermann* is F*cking Crazy!

Bitter, angry, unhinged Olbermann was impossible to work with, so the networks jettisoned and repackaged him as an angry outsider. The purpose of Olbermann's rambling, insane and now defunct internet show, "The Resistance"—a rip-off and obvious parody of *Infowars'* "Resistance"—was not only designed to discredit and make a mockery of Alex Jones, but has of course been used as an unassailable, plausible deniability platform from which to spew hatred and sling mud against Candidate, President-Elect and now President Trump. This is a strategy similarly employed by other MSM late night talk and comedy shows. We know who they are.

Olbermann's anger is real, because in all likelihood, Olbermann genuinely resented being fired from his network gigs. He wants more than anything to reacquire the *gravitas* of a national network anchor, but he's too volatile, unmanageable and anti-social for that–though, as this book and his podcasts show, he is, in his own twisted way, eloquent.

From the Establishment perspective, it's sinful to waste Olbermann's unique talents. Better to weaponize them into anti-Trump, anti-*Infowars*, anti-Deplorable glossolalia. Olbermann has been unleashed upon the American Public as a frothing rabid dog both to whip up the zombified legion of Anti-Trumpers, as well as provoke Trump Supporters into becoming angry and hopefully (this has not succeeded) violent in order to smear and discredit them. That, from the Establishment perspective, is putting Keith to good use.

That's why Olbermann unchained and uncensored on Youtube, where—unlike Deplorable content, or even that of ordinary conservatives—Olbermann's video content as well as his tweets, though chock-full of the worst vulgarity and threats of violence against President Trump, never get blocked or censored, and Olbermann is never suspended.This is because wittingly or not, Olbermann serves the Establishment's purpose.

Olbermann is simultaneously a Useful Idiot and Useful Mad Genius. Olbermann serves the Establishment but is forced to do so at the margins of respectability, as a *faux* rebel. A parody of a rebel. Why then is Trump, a man Olbermann clearly views as a charlatan, allowed to occupy the highest, most respected office in the land while he, Olbermann, a man fired from all his high-profile mainstream gigs, labors away in the internet salt mines? It fills him with rage. It drives him "f*cking crazy!" It underscores what a petty jerk Olbermann really is.

In the entire 400+ page rant of a book completely devoid of any journalistic integrity whatsoever, not once is there any criticism or suspicion cast upon Hillary, Obama, or the DC Establishment. Olbermann plays simplistic partisan politics: Good Democrats vs Evil Republicans. Though he often accuses President Trump of acting like a child, there's zero nuance to his completely wrongheaded, child-like arguments. Olbermann would have you think Republicans support Trump (only a handful of Deplorables do), when nothing could be more laughably further from the truth.

Olbermann is most rabid about #Russia

EVERY DAY we bring up Russia.
EVERY DAY we shout Russia!
EVERY DAY we SCREAM Russia

Olbermann, *Trump is F*cking Crazy*

HILLARY: "Will someone please shut this f*cking guy up, already!"

Olbermann's position on Trump, and his entire, breathless, white-knuckled 420 page-long rant of a book rests on a sum total of two claims, the pillars of which rest upon the shakiest of foundations:

    #1 Trump is crazy
    #2 Trump is a Russian Agent

We've already debunked claim #1 by concluding that Olbermann is projecting his own insanity on to Trump, so let's now turn our attention to claim #2: "Trump is a Russian Agent."

Starting at the most basic unit, what is Russia?

Olbermann appears to subscribe to the antiquated notion that the Russian Federation is only posing as the Russian Federation, when in fact it's still the Union of Soviet Socialist Republics *aka* the USSR. This was true from 1917 to 1989, but since then and after a rough 10-year transition period dominated by rapacious Globalist-sponsored Oligarchs throughout the 1990s, Boris Yeltsin, in what was likely a rare sober moment, in the year 2000 wisely and peacefully ceded the keys to the Russian kingdom to one Vladimir Vladimirovich Putin, who has led the country out of an 83+ year genocidal, communist nightmare and into sovereign, largely Christian territory.

In the past, I've written a good deal about Vladimir Putin, his merits as a leader and the many ways that the Russian Federation has enjoyed a steady, marked improvement in quality of life since he became President, so I won't go into that narrative at length here, but suffice it to say that though Russia pursues its own sovereign interests, those interests are largely, despite what the Globalists and NATO like to bleat about, in alignment with US interests. Trump understands this. Putin understands this. Both men would like nothing more than to form a partnership based on mutual respect and interests, but find it very difficult to do so when each of their own Globalist Deep States, in order to justify their own shaky existence, fight so bitterly against that ever happening. There's a long way to go before that happy day of mutual interest partnership can be realized, but just because both men would like it to happen doesn't mean that Trump is or ever has been a Russian Agent! Nor does this mean that Trump is some kind of useful idiot for Putin.

Trump is a patriot who believes in America First and understands he has much swamp draining to do before he can form a truly wide-reaching formal partnership with a sovereign, Christian, anti-Radical Islam Russia.

When Olbermann, his ilk on the Left and in the Mainstream media scream "Russia, Russia, Russia!" all day long, they fail to recognize what 2018 Russia actually is. Russia is not and likely never will ever again be anything like the USSR. Russia's goals of peace, prosperity, sovereignty, tradition, family, Christian values, Western Civilization, Renaissance, anti-New World Order, and anti-Globalism are values shared by most Americans and are exactly what Trump and his supporters cherish. And while just as there are bad Globalist Deep State actors in America, there are bad, Globalist Deep State actors in Russia. Neither Putin nor Trump are that.

So now that we have a handle on Russia, what about the claim that Trump is a Russian Agent?

Now more than one year into President Trump's term, with steady heat from the light of truth beating down hard upon the swamp water and bringing it to a roiling boil, it becomes increasingly clear that the only one who did not collude with Russia is Donald Trump!

With #PeepeeGateGPSFusion & #UraniumOne, all the guilt is on the side of the Globalists, starting at the top with Barack Obama! The legal team of Rosenstein & Mueller are also completely caught with their grubby hands in both those cookie jars. Other significant dirty pool players include but are not limited to: Hillary Clinton, Bill Clinton, James Comey, John Podesta, Tony Podesta, and John McCain.

"Wiretapping," a claim Trump made for which he was called crazy by Olbermann and everyone else in the Mainstream media, has been shown to be 100% true! This is because The PeepeeGate Steele Dossier (paid for by the FBI, Hillary Clinton and the DNC) was used as an illegal pretext to create a FISA warrant that led to the unwarranted surveillance and illegal unmasking by Susan Rice, Samantha Power and others that was in turn, by design, illegally leaked to the press. And once again, all signs point to the fact that this was done with the full knowledge of then-President Barack Hussein Obama – making this #Obamagate scandal of monumental proportions that needs, preferably through the formation of a second Special Counsel, to be investigated at once. The Nunes Memo was just the opening salvo.

Strange how there's not a single mention of any of these scandals in Olbermann's book...

Disoriented, disconnected, virtue-signaling Olbermann clearly doesn't understand that we're living in historic times, where the Globalist power structure, barely clinging to power by its fingernails, absorbs a devastating series of body blows. Will a head-shot even be necessary to finally bring it down?

Seeing the world exclusively through a Republican vs Democrat rather than Globalist vs Nationalist lens,

Olbermann doesn't appear to understand that Republicans are also against Trump; that the Establishment is the Establishment regardless of party affiliation.

Olbermann sees Trump vs Deep State in monolithic terms. Moreover, he fails to comprehend that there are many pro-Trump agents scattered throughout the Military, Intelligence Community and other government institutions (i.e. Q Anon). And it's many of those unsung, often times anonymous heroes who end up acting as sources for intrepid Citizen Journalists like Mike Cernovich, Jack Posobiec and Alex Jones.

If Olbermann, a man who has clearly abandoned any semblance of journalistic integrity is so smart, why does he seem so unwilling to engage in debate with Citizen Journalists? Afraid? Too much of an elitist? Both?

Olbermann is very careful these days to stay within his hermetically sealed echo chamber. If and when he dares dip his toe in public waters at all, it's to make a book-promoting appearance on softball shows like "The View." He knows he would wither and die within any serious debate format.

Olbermann actually seems to think that if the shoe was on the other foot—that if Globalist Deep State Hillary was the one (she actually is) guilty of "Russian" *aka* Globalist Deep State Russian (critical distinction) collusion—that the Republicans, those hapless cucked RINOS, would not stand for it! C'mon, Keith. Wise up.

Future generations will comfort themselves and move forward driven in part by the comfort of knowing that you, Paul Ryan, and you, Donald Trump, will burn in hell. Keith Olbermann, *Trump is F*cking Crazy*

Though the context of this quote was Olbermann making a lame reference to what he believes to be Trump and Ryan's shared support for coal mining, an industry Olbermann seems to believe is cruel and inhumane (that's actually a conversation worth exploring), what's most telling is how Olbermann really seems to believe that Ryan and Trump, two men who likely tolerate each other only because they have to, are in cahoots. I guess that's why Paul Ryan has recently announded his resignation as Speaker of the House. Because he gets on so well with Trump. Right.

The DNC is disintegrating, and the Establishment GOP is fast falling apart with them. The binary prism of bipartisan politics-as-usual has been shattered. Nevertheless, Trump did have to win over the GOP Establishment in order to get his legislation like the "Tax Cuts and Jobs Act" passed, so in that sense, I'll concede that there's a grain – but just a grain – of truth to what Olbermann's saying, but it's misleading.

In writing this chapter, it's finally dawned on me what the source of Keith Olbermann's insanity actually is. It's not just Donald Trump or *Trumpis* Envy—it's the fact that Olbermann and his fragile, hanging-by-a-thread worldview, cannot even remotely accept the existence of anything resembling a Globalist Deep State, let alone that the United States and any other country that cares about preserving its national sovereignty is in fact at war with this Globalist Deep State.

Whatever solidity Olbermann's psyche may have had left, the cognitive dissonance caused by this lack of recognition of Deep State reality has clearly pushed him off the cliff of sanity. Olbermann's following isn't as much an echo chamber as it is a padded room with a camera, microphone and keyboard.

So while Olbermann declares *ad infinitum*, "We're at war with Russia!" he completely misses the fact that it's actually the Globalist Deep State/New World Order he serves that is the avowed enemy of not just this country and all other countries, but of humanity itself. If Olbermann realized this, perhaps he would begin to understand what he's seeing around him and have no choice but to soften his stance against Trump. Instead, he overreacts to every paranoiac-perceived sleight, and with Pavlovian fury proceeds to foam at the mouth as he spreads his germ-ridden toxic hatred of all things true, good and Trump.

Olbermann and his feeble-minded, gullible acolytes are like cats to a light pointer whenever there's some news that they think might be even remotely negative about Trump. Funny thing is, nearly all the bad news that they so desperately wish to gloat over invariably turns out to be fake or just plain wrong.

In the first half of his book, Olbermann screams bloody murder about James Comey and his perfidiousness against Hillary right before the election. But that's all forgotten when Trump fires Comey. Suddenly Comey is, if not a great guy, the moral equivalent of the Rock of Gibraltar.

As mentioned, Hillary Clinton is for all intents and purposes an invisible figure in Olbermann's screed. So is Bill Clinton. So is John Podesta. Not even a whiff of suspicion about their clear and obviously nefarious activities.

Huma Abedin? Anthony Weiner? Lolita Express? Barack Obama? They similarly do not exist within the Olbermann Orbit.

Alternative media? Doesn't exist. Only *WaPo*, the *NYT* and other purely mainstream outlets exist.

No doubt Keith Olbemann has written a mean book about Trump. But should we cry about it? Absolutely not. Like Hillary Clinton and her many Globalist Deep State partners in crime, loser lefties like Olbermann do a great job of taking themselves down without any help from us Deplorables.

So rather than wasting precious energy getting angry at Keith Olbermann, I suggest having a seat, grabbing your popcorn and enjoying the spectacle of this highly entertaining tragicomic hit show, because...

...Olbermann Is F*cking Crazy.

9 The Wolff In Sheep's Clothing

Michael Wolff is a total loser who made up stories in order sell this really boring and untruthful book.

Donald Trump
Twitter, January 5, 2018

Though Michael Wolff's *Fire and Fury* is marketed as a Donald Trump book, Wolff and his publishers clearly and correctly understood that it would not sell anywhere near as many copies if it had been presented to the public for what it really is: a Steve Bannon book.

Fire and Fury, while a well written *albeit* fictitious page turner, is essentially a 300-page gossip column.

The only fleshed out (pun intended) character, since he seems to have been the sole person with whom Wolff enjoyed any form of consistent access, was Bannon. Everyone else, and none more so than Trump, is painted with the broadest possible strokes.

Fire and Fury can also be viewed as the literary equivalent to one of the many hackneyed Alec Baldwin/Trump *Saturday Night Live* skits and just about as credible.

Though exceedingly loose with the facts, Wolff is a talented writer not lacking in ability to keep the readers' interest. Unlike the President, bored by the read I was not.

To Wolff's credit, *Fire and Fury* does offer some keen insights on what no doubt at times appears to be the controlled chaos that is the Trump White House, particularly the interplay between the polar opposites that was at the time of the book's composition the three-headed Hydra of Jarvanka (Jared and Ivanka Trump), former Chief Strategist Steve Bannon and former White House Chief of Staff Reince Priebus. That said, in fairness to Jarvanka and Priebus, with almost no direct quotes from any of them, we really don't receive their version of events, thus rendering their characterization highly suspect.

Bannon however is a different story. There's no book without Bannon. Quoted extensively, Bannon's portrayal appears to have been fairly accurate. Additionally, the fact that he offered no denial of anything he's quoted as saying speaks volumes. Clearly Bannon expected the book to help not hurt him, but as we all now know, that's not quite how it all turned out. So why did Bannon allow this to happen?

My take? Bannon outsmarted himself and this Wolff in Sheep's Clothing took full advantage of his golden goose. And let's face it, how could he not?

Bannon clearly thought he could use Wolff not only to get his Nationalist message out, one that he knew most Deplorables—including myself—agreed with, but also, most importantly, to promote himself as the sole architect of that message, as the *auteur* of the Deplorable Movement, and as Trump's brain. Never mind the fact that as we discussed in the Bannon chapter, Trump has been crafting his America First message for decades, or that Stephen Miller (who Wolff falsely and tellingly dismisses as "Bannon's typist") was the one writing Candidate and President Trump's most impactful, anti-Globalist, pro-Nationalist speeches. No, no, no. Bannon fully intended to use Wolff in order to delegitimize Trump; to make the President look foolish, petty, incompetent and dangerously crazy. This "best laid plan of mice and men," as we all now know, ended up backfiring badly.

Bannon, someone who should've known better, learned a hard lesson. When you take your shot, you best not miss. Bannon missed. Now he's been deservedly exiled and will probably never return. He even earned a permanent nickname: #Sloppy Steve.

Like the cat who knows just where to find a room full of spilled milk, one can hardly blame Wolff for lapping all this up. He was clever. When nearly everyone else in the Mainstream media was roasting Bannon over the coals for being a racist and White Supremacist (totally untrue, but that's just how it was), Wolff seemed to have gained Bannon's confidence with a puff piece in a November 2016 *Hollywood Reporter* article, *Ringside with Steve Bannon*, that allowed Bannon free rein to lay out his platform. That article seemed to have gained Wolff the key to the White House Kingdom. And though Wolff now admits there were never any interviews with the President or any members of his Cabinet other than Steve Bannon. Wolff managed to scoop up just enough stray crumbs from the table for him to construct his assigned anti-Trump narrative.

To no one's great surprise, as the release date loomed and Wolff hit the MSM news and talk show circuit, he couldn't emphasize enough how non-partisan and objective his take was. Only problem was that everything he had to say about Trump was so completely negative, that his claims of being an objective observer were laughable.

When you read *Fire and Fury*, Wolff's anti-Trump politics are crystal clear on such events as Russia Collusion (now proven non-existent by the lack of any corroborating evidence found as a result of the Mueller indictments), the Mueller Special Counsel, General Flynn, Syria, Wiretapping, Charlottesville, the Paris Climate Accords, cutting Regulations (Wolff says nothing), and the booming Economy (Wolff says nothing). Wolff's commentary on these events rarely contains any balanced context, thus demonstrating the author's clear Anti-Trump bias that he so vehemently but unconvincingly attempts to deny during his dog and pony show with the Mainstream media.

Wolff's primary Deep State and Bannon-channeled thesis is that Trump is dangerously crazy and borderline 25th Amendment crazy. As potentially harmful to national interests as that false claim is, Wolff is not exactly acting as an outlier here, since it's been an opposition talking point for months. Important to keep in mind that Trump's perfect 30 out of 30 score on his mental health test pretty much put the nail in the coffin on this now-debunked *"Trump's Crazy"* meme.

Wolff's more outrageous claim—possibly via Bannon—is: Trump never wanted or intended to win the election. The idea here is that Trump wanted to get close enough to winning to bolster his already successful brand, but not to actually win, because he didn't actually want be President. Ok...

Did Trump think being President would be too difficult for him? That seems out of character.

Was Trump really not about winning? He's been more demonstrably about winning than nearly anyone on the planet, so that also seems unlikely.

From the beginning of the campaign, whenever he was asked about his chances of winning, Trump never failed to say, and it's totally credible, *"I'd never run if I didn't think I could win."* The results do appear to have borne this out.

Let's also remember that before getting close enough to sniff the ultimate prize (that Wolff claims Trump didn't actually want), he first had to defeat 16 (that's *sixteen* with an "S") other GOP candidates in the Republican primaries, including the Big GOP donor-anointed Jeb Bush, who nearly all the pundits were saying (because they knew what was planned) that a Bush/Clinton general election race was a done deal. *Fait accomplit.*

And yet Donald Trump comes along to completely upset that applecart. Quite the Herculean accomplishment for a man who doesn't want to win. So...there's that.

Now how about those who say he wanted to get close enough to improve his brand but not actually win?

Since when is losing—any type of losing—better for one's brand than winning? Never! Winning is always better. It's the best. And Trump, who even his critics would say is nothing if not a man of unabashed superlatives would never settle for losing when, running against such a thoroughly corrupt, terrible candidate like Hillary Clinton. Clearly from Donald Trump's perspective, though victory was by no means assured, he knew better than to underestimate Deep State power to defraud the public. From Trump's point of view, defeating Hillary was not only possible, it was probable. And that mentality prevailed despite his knowing how rigged in Hillary's favor the 2016 election truly was.

And again, from a branding perspective, is there anything better for the Trump brand in the long-term than being President of the world's #1 brand: USA? I don't think so.

And finally, if you're responsible for actually making America great again, it's a total Branding Home Run!

Michael Wolff, Ladies and Gentlemen, though a clever con artist, artful weaver of tall tales, and borderline marketing genius with plenty of chutzpah, is not only bald-*headed*, but also a bald-*faced* liar.

<u>Postscript</u>: It didn't take long for author Michael Wolff to wear out his welcome with an initially fawning Mainstream media. Less than a month after <u>Fire and Fury</u> was released, on February 1st, 2018, Wolff was unceremoniously booted off the set of MSNBC's <u>Morning Joe</u> by none other than the show's hostess, the rabidly anti-Trump Mika Brzezinski (daughter of now-deceased arch-Globalist Zbigniew Brzezinski), for insinuating without any evidence whatsoever that President Trump was having an affair with U.N. Ambassador Nikki Haley. But it gets better.

A few weeks later, when prompted during an Australian television interview to issue an apology to the President for those same unfounded claims of having an affair with Haley, Wolff panicked as he suddenly began indicating to the show's producer that his earpiece was malfunctioning, he couldn't hear the question and could no longer continue the interview, as he walked off the set. Aaaaand...scene.

Deplorables are unified around a love of country: MAGA, while Trump detractors are hopelessly fractured by self-loathing.

                Mac Balzac, Twitter, August 21, 2017

II

Deplorables Rising

10 Deplorable State of the Union

Like much of the public, I saw a scary extremism in Trump's language and policy preferences during the campaign. But I recognized his hyperbole as weapons-grade persuasion that would change after the election, not a sign that Trump had suddenly turned into Hitler.

Scott Adams, Win Bigly

In a recent podcast, Scott Adams, creator of *Dilbert* and author of the definitive book on Donald Trump's mastery of persuasion, *Win Bigly*, raised a critical point on how there are typically two phases to building a building: Demolition and Construction.

Before Donald Trump could really start fulfilling his 5 Key Campaign Promises: Make America Great Again (MAGA), America First, Build The Wall, Drain The Swamp, and Lock Her Up!, he needed a clean, empty lot.

Here's a 22-point list of just some of the old pillars of the Establishment that President Trump has largely demolished since the Campaign:

- The Democratic Party
- The Republican Establishment
- The Bush Dynasty
- The Clinton Dynasty
- Pollsters
- The Mainstream media
- Hollywood Celebrity Culture
- Obamacare

- Obama Executive Orders
- Barack Obama's legacy
- Political Correctness
- Regulations
- The Trans Pacific Partnership (TPP)
- The Paris Climate Accords
- ISIS
- China Policy
- North Korea Policy
- NAFTA Policy
- Human Trafficking Policy
- Immigration Policy
- Energy Policy
- Liberal Dominance of the Supreme Court

That's what the President has largely destroyed. Now let's take a look at what he's been able to build by fulfilling his campaign promises during his first year in office:

We've got a President in office for six months who's accomplished nothing. Debbie Wasserman Schultz, CNN, June 22, 2017

Nothing, Deb? *Really?* The facts speak for themselves. I suggest getting your own scandal-ridden glass house in order before throwing stones.

Trump has crushed it on the Economy, Foreign Policy, National Security, Energy and the Culture War, so it's no surprise that the Establishment has sought to downplay Trump's many, and to my mind unprecedented list of accomplishments in a mere 15 months in office.

Here's my compilation of President Trump's **Accomplishments**. Spoiler Alert: it's long!

Economy (14):
- Stock Market continues to break record highs gaining over $2 trillion in wealth, and the S&P broke over $20 trillion for the fist time in its history.
- Unemployment at a 16-year low. Lowest rate since 2001. Trump has decreased unemployment rate every month since taking office.
- Black Unemployment at an all-time low.
- Strong rebound in confidence in the US economy via effective application of *The Power of Positive Thinking*. (author Dale Carnegie was a Trump mentor).
- Trump created nearly 1 million new jobs in his first four months in office, while Obama lost more than 3 million jobs in his first four months, causing POTUS 44 to say, "Jobs are never coming back."
- TPP withdrawal.
- US Manufacturing Index at a 33-year high.
- Signing of the "Buy American, Hire American" Initiative.
- GDP rises from 1.5% in 2016 to 2.3% in 2017.
- Housing Sales are red-hot.
- Greatly increased Consumer Confidence.
- Passage of the Tax Cuts and Jobs Act.
- Tariffs placed on Aluminum and Steel imports; a clear sign of an "America First" return to fair, protectionist policies that boost American manufacturing.
- $60 billion tariff on China for theft of United States intellectual property.

Foreign Policy (15):
- Under extreme pressure from effective US-led sanctions, Kim Jong Un agrees to denuclearize, meets with S Korean President Moon on S Korean soil and is scheduled to soon meet face-to-face with President Trump to ink an historic peace treaty.
- Two Syria Missile Strikes.
- Peace Deal in southern Syria with Russia and Jordan.
- Strengthening of Relations with China garners more respect from Chinese leadership. Trump praises Chinese President Xi for his essential leadership in helping bring all parties together.
- Crushing ISIS.
- Arab Summit calms tensions in the Middle East. Helps usher in new reformist leadership in Saudi Arabia.
- "Meet Financial Obligations" speech to NATO substantially increases member defense spending.
- Strengthening relations with India.
- Visit to France bolsters relations between France and the United States when most assumed the election of Globalist Emmanuel Macron would worsen ties.
- Ending CIA program to arm Syrian "Rebels (ISIS)
- Pulling billions in funding to the UN.
- UN Speech on the critical importance of National Sovereignty.
- East Asian Tour which solidified US relations with Japan, South Korea, China, Vietnam & The Phillipines.
- US Embassy moves from Tel Aviv to Jerusalem.
- Pro National Sovereignty speech at Davos.

National Security (12):
- Travel Ban.
- National Guard ordered to deploy to southern border.
- Thousands of Human Trafficking Arrests.
- Ending of "Catch and Release" Immigration policy.
- Reduction of border crossings by 73%.
- ICE has made over 40,000 arrests.
- Passage of "Kate's Law" which increases penalties for previously deported criminals.
- Passage of the "No Sanctuary for Criminals Act" which punishes Sanctuary Cities.
- Refugee intake reduced over 50%.
- Sending of Federal Government Personnel to Chicago to help reduce record-level crime.
- Passage of the "Reforming American Immigration for Strong Emplyment Act" (RAISE).
- Calls for an end to Chain Migration. Implements a Merit Based Immigration System. Offers a 12 year path to citizenship and comprehensive plan for DACA.

Energy (7):
- $100 Million to Flint Water Crisis.
- Paris Climate Change withdrawal.
- Coal Industry reopens for business.
- Initiated construction of Keystone & Dakota Energy Pipelines.
- Stabilization and decline in Gas Prices due to increase in domestic production.
- Sale of American-made energy to Poland.
- Commitment to eliminating oil imports and establishing American energy independence.

Government/Bureaucracy (11):
- For every one regulation, two must go.
- Trump cut $22 billion in new regulations in his first five months, while Obama added $3 billion in new regulations.
- 5-year Lobbying Ban for all departing members of Congress and their staff.
- Approval of Trump administration policies leading to most State Special Elections being won by GOP.
- Signing of 13 CRAs (Congressional Review Acts).
- Signing of 30 new Executive Orders.
- Eliminating many Executive Orders signed by Obama.
- Signing of 40 new bills into law.
- Cutting of wasteful government staffing requirements which has saved millions of dollars.
- Elimination of the Obamacare Mandate.
- Causing Chuck Schumer and the Democrats to blink on Government Shutdown.

Personnel (21):
- Appointment of SCOTUS Neil Gorsuch.
- Nomination of 31 new Federal Judges.
- Anthony "Mooch" Scaramucci replaces Sean Spicer as head of WH Communications.
- Mooch goes nuts and fired 10 days later.
- Sara Huckabee Sanders appointed as full-time Press Secretary role. She rocks!
- Firing of GOPe insider, Chief of Staff Reince Priebus.
- Appointment of General John Kelly as Chief of Staff.
- FBI Director Jim Comey fired.
- Christopher Wray appointed FBI Director.
- Steve Bannon resigns with Trump's blessing.
- White House Counterterrorism Adviser Sebastian Gorka resigns.
- Globalist Deputy National Security Advisor Dina Powell fired.
- Richard Grenfell (finally) named German Ambassador
- Chief Economic Officer "Globalist" Gary Cohn resigns.
- Secretary of State Rex Tillerson fired.
- Mike Pompeo named Secretary of State.
- Gina Haspel named CIA Director. First female CIA Director in US history
- Assistant FBI Director Andrew McCabe fired.
- Larry Kudlow hired as Chief Economic Advisor.
- General H.R. McMaster fired as NSC Director.
- John Bolton hired as NSC Director.

Culture War (15):
- Calls out CNN "You are Fake News!" at press conference.
- CNN/MSM Meme War.
- Fake News Awards.
- Melania Trump's pre-Rally Speech Prayer.
- Exposes fact that 17 Intel Agencies do NOT all agree on Russia Collusion.
- Although he's no longer in the government, Sebastian Gorka emerges as an articulate voice of the Deplorable Movement.
- Warsaw "Defense of the West" Speech.
- 45,000 attend Boy Scout Jamboree Speech.
- Military Transgender Ban.
- Ending of Taxpayer funding of Abortion.
- Within an hour of the outbreak of violence in Charlottesville, Trump condemned the political violence from both sides.
- Trump calls out Alt-Left violence.
- Trump questions the logic of removing Confederate statues and monuments.
- Criticism of the NFL.
- Demonstration of master-level Twitter Persuasion Game.

That's an 95-point list, folks. Only five shy of ONE HUNDRED points.

And though he gets criticized by his enemies for not getting enough legislation passed, it's not making excuses to point out that the Democrats have not lifted a finger to help, acting as pure obstructionists at every turn.

Meanwhile, as we saw with healthcare, key members of the GOP like John McCain are determined to cock-block Trump whenever they can. The President has spoken of having hundreds of pieces of legislation ready to send to Congress but is no doubt wary of watching that legislation get shot down by those same dishonest, obstructive Democrats and RINOs. Success in the 2018 Midterm elections will be key to Draining the Swamp in Congress and getting more America First legislation passed.

Despite all the MAGA and America First accomplishments listed above, Deep State MSM, the cucked GOPe and the Left continue to focus on Trump's fake low poll numbers (though the latest Rasmussen poll shows Trump at 52%, which is still probably 10-15 points lower than it actually is, demonstrating that he's only gaining in popularity).

Trump's political enemies have worked overtime to thwart passage of healthcare legislation, beat the dead horse of "Russia Collusion," collude on the conflict-of-interest-laden Special Counsel, and continue to fan the flames of the failure to pass healthcare legislation, and finally the "Trump is a Racist" meme that was reignited by the President's (very fair and reasonable handling of) the violence coming out of Charlottesville.

The good news is, the majority of the American people are seeing right through these shenanigans. I expect it all to backfire on Deep State as POTUS' agenda continues to be more and more fulfilled. Corrupt, obstructionist Democrat incumbents and corrupt, cucked Establishment Republican incumbents get voted out, and all that dead wood is replaced by up-and-coming Deplorable politicians.

If this Presidency is like a boxing match, having only completed 13 months of the first term of his Presidency (yes, I'm counting my chickens a bit...), that's only about 15% of the term, which would equate to only two rounds of a full 12-round fight. This is why Trump is still mainly throwing stiff jabs and body shots rather than haymakers. He's feeling his opponent out. POTUS knows it's a long fight and he must proceed with savvy, intelligence and strategy. You can't take Deep State lightly!

Personnel is Policy

Though not entirely his fault, Trump's worst area of performance would be his personnel handling. "Personnel is Policy," and a failure to both inject the administration with massive numbers of Trump Loyalists while at the same time purging it of Obama and Bush holdovers has hampered the President's progress in multiple areas.

Replacing wrongly accused patriot General Flynn, with Globalist General McMaster was detrimental to MAGA. McMaster removed from NSC nearly all its Nationalist Trump Supporters and replaced them with Globalists like (recently fired) Dina Powell and Fiona Hill. Newly appointed NSC Director Bolton does appear set to clean house, so let's see how that plays out.

Most of the federal bureaucracy still consists of 80% Obama and Bush holdovers. *Eighty percent!* That fact, coupled with an unconstitutional domestic NSA spying program have been big reasons why leaks have been a major problem, and POTUS continues to receive massive amounts of pushback on every populist proposal he makes. It's truly remarkable that he's still been able to accomplish so much of the MAGA and America First agenda while being literally surrounded and often isolated by the enemy.

Draining The Swamp

So why aren't the Committees, investigators, and of course our beleaguered A.G., looking into Crooked Hillary's crimes & Russia relations?

> Donald Trump
> Twitter, July 24, 2017

Perhaps the President's allies in the government are beginning to listen.

The House Judiciary committee is calling for (let's hope they follow through) the formation of a Special Counsel(s) along with more federal investigations to look into the many actual crimes committed by Obama, the Clintons, the Podestas, Comey, McCabe, Lynch, Rice, Power, Brennan, Clapper, Holder, McCain, Kerry, Mills, Wasserman-Schultz, Abedin and Weiner.

According to *Fox News*, the House Judiciary Committee "delivered an extensive, 14-point request for what a second Special Counsel should cover." This includes but is not limited to:

- Allegations that former Attorney General Loretta Lynch instructed then-FBI Director James Comey to downplay the nature of the Clinton email probe
- The FBI and DOJ's decisions in the course of the email probe, including controversial immunity deals with Clinton aide Cheryl Mills and others
- The State Department's involvement in deciding which Clinton emails to make public
- Disclosures in *WikiLeaks*-released emails regarding the Clinton Foundation and "its potentially unlawful international dealings"
- Connections between Clinton officials and "foreign entities" including Russia and Ukraine
- Revelations in hacked Democratic National Committee emails about "inappropriate" coordination between the DNC and Clinton campaign against Bernie Sanders' Democratic primary campaign
- The "unmasking" of Americans in intelligence documents and potentially related leaks of classified information
- Comey's admitted leak of details of his conversations with President Trump
- The FBI's "reliance" on controversial firm Fusion GPS involved in the questionable anti-Trump "dossier" paid for by Hillary and the DNC, aided and abetted by RINO John McCain and facilitated by the Obama DOJ and FBI to get approval for a FISA Warrant to spy on Trump, his associates and transition team.

According to a recent *Infowars* report from Dr. Jerome Corsi, Hillary has apparently been offered a plea deal for the email scandal. That's huge. It shows real mounting pressure on Bill, Huma Abedin, Anthony Weiner and John Podesta in Clinton Foundation and Pay-for-Play scandals.

While we're all still waiting for investigations to begin, it's clear (even *CNN* now reports it) that Trump was 100% correct in pointing out that he was being "wiretapped." And after he was spied upon, Rice and others like Sally Yates from DOJ and Samantha Power from the UN leaked hundreds of unmasked names to sources in the Mainstream media. I'm looking forward to the formation of a second Special Counsel (or the legal equivalent) that has the power to start issuing subpoenas and indictments to the entire criminal cabal, and it needs to happen ASAP.

The baseless witch hunt that is the Mueller Special Counsel has already vastly exceeded the narrow scope of its "Russian Interference" mandate. Framing General Flynn, indicting a handful of Russian Internet trolls, indicting Paul Manafort on financial issues unrelated to the campaign and getting a FISA warrant to spy on one of the FBI's own undercover employees in Carter Page is the sum total of what the Mueller Special Counsel has amounted to. A total fraud!

General Flynn's admission of lying to the FBI will likely be thrown out and his case dismissed because the tape used to generate the confession was created by unlawful means ("fruit of the poison tree") and the FBI "302" form which gave a description of the crime was likely doctored, by recently fired former FBI Assistant Director Andrew McCabe.

The Left would love to see the President fire Mueller (so that it could try to lay an Obstruction of Justice charge on the President), but why throw gasoline on the fire when the Mueller investigation is doing such a great job of exposing (however inadvertently) real criminals like Andrew McCabe, Peter Strozk, Sally Yates, Susan Rice and the many conflict-of-interest laden members of the Special Counsel including Robert Mueller himself. Any investigation of Uranium One, and this appears to be coming down the pike, will likely expose serious criminality perpetrated by the "Three Amigos:" Rod Rosenstein, Robert Mueller and James Comey.

Now that we're in counterattack mode, it's vital for Attorney General Jeff Sessions to start forming those new special counsels and issuing indictments that could lead to military tribunal trials. While many in the MSM and Senate criticized the President for giving Sessions a hard time, all the Deplorables I know totally agree with Trump for stepping up pressure on what has thus far been a very weak, underwhelming performance by our "beleaguered" Attorney General.

While I do realize that there's likely enormous pressure from multiple Deep State sources for Sessions not to indict the criminals, since that criminality runs so pervasively throughout the Duopoly, by bringing those swamp creatures to justice, the entire House of Cards could come down. Good! That's what "Drain The Swamp" means. If Sessions can't do it, he needs to be replaced. My gut tells me Sessions (though Deep State likely has dirt on him) is slow-walking the perps and will do what needs to be done, but the clock is ticking.

My Solution to the Donald Trump White House Personnel Dilemma

If you throw a dog twenty Frisbees at the same time, he can only catch one at a time, and chances are he'll miss all of them because he won't be able to choose which one to target.
Stefan Molyneux

Not unlike Molyneux, I favor a Black Monday blitzkrieg approach to the President's personnel problem, finding the situation similar to dealing with minor civil procedures. Why rely on one argument when you can hit your opponent with 20—and all at the same time?! The result of this strategy has invariably been either outright dismissal or an offer to negotiate a reasonable settlement. Either way it's a win.

The idea then would be to hit Deep State all at once with the following announcements:

- Assange pardoned
- Mueller indicted
- Rosenstein fired
- Comey indicted
- McCabe indicted
- Hillary indicted
- Abedin indicted
- Weiner indicted
- Rice indicted
- Lynch indicted
- Clapper indicted
- Brennan indicted
- Obama indicted

How will MSM and the Political Establishment be able to effectively deal with these crushing announcements if all are made at the same time? Comical. They can't and they won't. It'll be downright comical! They'll trip all over themselves!

Dripping out each announcement one-by-one makes it way too easy for Trump's enemies. So why do it that way? Realistically, though it's highly unlikely that my solution would ever actually be employed, it should be! At least some of these pardons, firings and indictments should happen at the same time. I'd be thrilled with even three at once!

There are capable Trump loyalists with extensive government experience locked-and-loaded and ready to serve the President by filling the many positions currently inhabited by Obama holdovers. Time to get those folks in there!

Media Strategy

From a political warfare perspective, control of the news cycle is the most potent means of attracting and building up a favorable audience. Rich Higgins, *POTUS and Political Warfare*

Charlottesville was the proof in the pudding that it's high time for President Trump to move on from the habit of feeling that he still needs MSM to disseminate his message. I know he's the greatest Mainstream media troll on the planet, but all they'll ever do is attack him and his policies, and then spin, filter and dilute his message. Keep them on their heels!

To a certain extent, although it's a dangerous game, Trump trolls his political enemies in order to build his own brand. A man without enemies is a man without character.

Trump does however need to keep in mind the fact that in order to maintain the momentum that he knows is so important to successfully completing his promises to the American people, he must drive the media cycle every day. Utilizing social media and citizen journalism, he can do just that.

Half the country voted for Trump, and despite the continued practice of publishing fake, dishonest polls, Trump's unprecedented productivity as President has only served to widen his base. It's critical to keep that momentum going in order to push out more Dems and RINOS and replace them with Deplorable candidates in the 2018 Midterm Elections and beyond.

Let's all keep in mind that we're barely more than a year into the Trump Presidency. While Deep State will continue to do all it can to remove Trump, and there will be bumps in the road, I expect our victories to far outnumber our losses. The more time that passes and the list of POTUS' accomplishments continue to grow, we'll see more and more of the following:

- Prosperity increasing. US currently enjoys 2.3% GDP growth and expected to be closer to 3% by end of 2018.
- Increased awareness of the importance of maintaining National Sovereignty will be more pronounced and become more important to a majority of the American people.
- American optimism will continue to swell.
- Domestic enemies will begin to dwindle and grow weaker as they realize they're better off hopping on the Trump Train than getting run over by the Populist Revival.

- International Relations will continue to improve.
- National Security will increase as our borders become more secure & immigration policy more rational.
- The Republic will be restored.

The battle against Deep State is ongoing. While the Democrats and Social Justice Warriors (SJWs) are obvious enemies who former White House Communications Director Anthony Scaramucci would describe as "front-stabbers," the GOP Establishment, Cuckservatives and GOP Neocons are the more insidious backstabbers operating from the shadows who not only threaten Trump but undermine the entire Deplorable Movement. They need to be exposed, indicted (where applicable), voted out and removed.

It's important to keep in mind that Deep State agencies and its many bureaucrats both in government and the private sector are in a constant battle to justify their increasingly irrelevant existence. False Flags will likely increase as Deep State fights to remain relevant, but it's more an indication of their death rattle than anything else. This is why we have false flag events such as mass shootings like we've recently seen in Las Vegas, Parkland and others that proceeded them.

The FBI hasn't been relevant for decades and was probably never necessary in the first place. The ultimate Fake News outlet, *CNN* leads the charge in the coverage of false flags like Parkland, and they are bleeding viewers. Nevertheless, look at how Deep State has been able to take over the news cycle from a winning Donald Trump since that event took place. Gun Control is not the issue here.

Deep State faces an existential crisis and will stoop to the lowest levels, including allowing (or actively participating in) the mass murder of children if it means they don't have to shut their doors. Never forget that fact.

Don't Just Be a Trump Cheerleader

Some Deplorables who feel very protective of the President wish to shield him from criticism from the Base, fearing it's a sign of disloyalty. They only want to tell him how great he is and how wonderful a job is doing. That's a dangerous approach. We always need to call things as they are, and not how we'd like them to be.

President Trump does not need an army of cheerleaders, sheep and Yes Men. He needs discerning warriors adept at seeing through the illusions and spin coming from the Deep State enemy. The news isn't always good. Sometimes battles are lost. Rather than delude ourselves into thinking they don't exist, we need to accept those losses and keep moving forward with the agenda. Losses are a part of life. Failing to provide the necessary honest feedback to the President can induce him to make incorrect decisions based on misleading information from the grassroots.

Unlike in previous decades, Deep State no longer enjoys *carte blanche* to engage in its nefarious, treasonous activities. We live in the Golden Age of Information and Information Warfare. That's why Deep State is doing everything it possibly can to censor and shut down citizen journalism and social media. But to achieve their objective, only totalitarianism allows them to gain full spectrum dominance, and Deplorables won't stand for it.

11 Trump is Who the Globalists Wanted is *Totally Wrong!*

Political warfare is warfare. Strategic information campaigns designed to delegitimize through disinformation arise out of non-violent lines of effort in political warfare regimes. They principally operate through narratives.

Rich Higgins
POTUS and Political Warfare

Is Donald Trump who the Globalist Elite really wanted to win the 2016 US Presidential election? Believe it or not, there are many in the Alternative media who believe this to be true. I don't, but let's take a few moments to drill down into what may be going on here.

Before attempting to answer the question of whether Trump was "who the Globalists wanted," it's important to ask whether this was a real question asked by real pundits – who in my opinion got it wrong—or was it actually a Deep State disinformation campaign designed to cast doubt on the legitimacy of a Trump Presidency? While we may never know for sure, my guess is that it's a bit of both.

David Icke, the "Classic Coke" of conspiracy theorists who I love and respect, is unable to fathom the possibility that Trump is not in the pocket of the Globalists. According to Icke's world view, if you play the political game, you have to be owned by someone. And particularly if you're running for President of the United States, it would be impossible not to be compromised by those willing to contribute the enormous amounts of money needed to run for political office. Additionally, to have a true reformer/system buster appear on the scene does not fit the Icke narrative that Globalists are essentially omniscient and invincible.

The cynicism derived from such a perspective and the sense of hopelessness that accompanies it not only plays right into the hands of the Globalist Establishment but is clearly a flaw in Icke's system of thought. I get it though, because there has been little in the form of precedence for Trump. We may have to go as far back as the Coolidge administration of the 1920s or perhaps even Andrew Jackson nearly 200 years earlier to find appropriate comparisons in American history.

While it's our duty as American citizens to hold Trump's feet to the fire in case he goes sideways (he would expect nothing less), we've already seen several indications, particularly in the area of personnel, where he appears to have attempted to appease the Globalists, i.e. H.R. McMaster, Dina Powell, Gary Cohn, Rex Tillerson... But notice after abouyt a year...Poof! All gone.

It's my view that President Trump will continue to be our best hope for true reform and Globalist system busting as he rolls back plans for the New World Order, ends a foreign policy of regime change, pulls back from the UN and continues to usher in a period of peace and prosperity that fosters an American Renaissance. This is happening!

And yet I'm sure David Icke and others like Brandon Smith from Alt-market.com, the writer who penned an article that was published in *Zerohedge* at the end of December 2016 entitled "Trump Is Exactly Where The Elites Want Him" will continue to doggedly cling to the idea that it's the Elite puppet masters who are pulling the strings, when in fact they're actually in full retreat and panic mode.

I have seen endless theories over the past several months on all the ways in which the global elites would sabotage the Trump campaign. I believe the phrase "they will never allow him to win" was repeated in nearly every discussion on the election. The assumption in this instance was that Trump is "anti-establishment" and, therefore, a threat to the globalists.

These are the same globalists that people also claimed would "rig the election," or initiate a "coup" in the electoral college to stop a Trump presidency. Of course, this never happened. So, a large percentage of the movement needs to question— why didn't it happen? How did Trump win within a system we know has been rigged for decades?" Brandon Smith, *Zerohedge*

Didn't happen? Deep State *did* rig the election, and it did atempt to undermine the electoral college, and, will continue doing all they can to initiate a coup in a desperate attempt to stop the President.

The extraordinary efforts to derail Trump have been unprecedented. Not a single Globalist wanted a Trump win. The entire Mainstream media was and still is completely against him. The leaders of most if not all of the intelligence agencies were and still are against him. The Democratic Party? Completely against him. The GOP Establishment? Completely against him (although he did manage to win some over with his Tax Cuts and Jobs Act). The EU is against him. The Chinese Deep State is against him. The Saudi Deep State is against him. The Federal Reserve is against him. The UN is against him. None of those entities wanted Trump to win and are stiff fighing with everything they have left to prevent that from becoming a reality. Proof of this was evident during the election and has only intensified post-election.

This is not mere paranoia. It's reality. The rigging was simply not enough to counter a truly populist movement.

Was Hillary Clinton in on the "charade?"

My point then as well as now is that without Clinton as the counter-party, Trump would not have garnered the political following he did. Any other Democratic candidate would not have galvanized conservatives so fervently. Smith, *Zerohedge*

This is even more ridiculous than Michael Wolff's claims in *Fire and Fury* that "Trump didn't want to win," and "Melania was devastated when he won." While I agree that Hillary was a terrible candidate, why, if she was hand-picked to lose, was she so sure that she would win? Why did *Newsweek* pre-print and dedicate an entire issue to "Madame President?" By hook or by crook, Hillary was going to be President! Only a popular and electoral landslide prevented that from happening.

Furthermore, Trump would likely have won not only against Hillary, but anyone else the Globalists would've backed, because 63+ million Deplorables had already awoken to the Globalist fraud. Trump understands that he's the *de facto* head of a Movement, and his victory was not merely the result of some kind of cult of personality.

And if Hillary was merely playing the part of a narcissistic, out-of-touch, arrogant, certain winner, she deserves an Oscar! Not buying it. Impossible. She's not that talented of an actress. No, the entire Establishment was banking on a Hillary win and was certain they had it sewn up and in the bag. But they didn't! They failed. They're in shock. They're on the run.

Everything that's happened since the election: the failed recount, the "Insurance Policy" illegal spying, the unmasking, the Russia Collusion charges, the formation of the Special Counsel, the Trump's Crazy meme, the Trump's a Racist meme, the Trump's a Sexual Harasser meme – all tried and all failed. Why bother if "Trump is who the Globalist Elite wanted?" Because the election of Donald Trump was the ultimate spanner in the Globalist System's machine. A total, perhaps fatal disaster.

Just like Hillary believed her own bullshit, the Globalists arrogantly believed theirs. Why else would they risk installing a man like Trump into office who has the potential of causing a Tsunami capable of washing away the entire New World Order?

They would never take such a risk if they thought it to be a risk; not because they controlled Trump, but because they felt they were firmly in control of everything and everyone else! They were so smug, so overconfident and so full of hubris, believing they could—as they've done now for a very long time—place their puppet in power.

Draining The Swamp

The first and worst sign that Trump is not anywhere near "anti-establishment" has been his complete reversal of his original "drain the swamp" rhetoric. Trump is not only NOT draining the swamp that is the Washington D.C. and corporate elitist revolving door, he is adding even more creatures of varying ghoulishness.

Smith, Zerohedge

"Draining the Swamp" requires a strategic, nuanced approach. To achieve prosperity, we need great business minds. It just so happens that Goldman Sachs, as the world's premier investment house, tends to attract such minds. Is it possible that a man like former WH Economic Advisor Globalist Gary Cohn was a globalist mole? In Gary's case, for sure. Trump believes that those who he's brought into his cabinet will serve his goal of creating prosperity for the nation. And if there's double-crossing from any of these appointees, they'll be shown the door, i.e. Reince Priebus Sean Spicer, James Comey, Steve Bannon. Rex Tillerson, H.R. McMaster, Dina Powell *et al.*

"Draining the Swamp" will also mean investigations and indictments of Deep State-corrupted bureaucrats at all levels of the government and throughout every institution. This will include clearing out the pedophiles and cleaning up the child trafficking cesspool that for years has been used as leverage to keep politicians toeing the Globalist line and anti-Globalists out of the game. An unprecedented number of Human Trafficking arrests have already been a hallmark of the Trump Administration, and I expect this trend to not only continue but increase exponentially.

The Fear-Mongering Myth of Economic Collapse

A big part of the power the Globalists seem to have over sovereign nations and their citizens is the threat of "economic collapse" that they constantly dangle over our heads like Damocles' Sword. Meanwhile, old-guard conspiracy theorists unwittingly play right into the Globalists' hand with their own fear-mongering cries of "Economic collapse!"

We are building a national economic/financial architecture in this country that will be largely immune from Globalist-dominated financial contagions. Since Donald Trump took office, job growth is way, up, optimism is high and the stock market is booming. The Trump American Economic System—based on principles that are as American as Jazz—relies on American ingenuity and creativity. If President Trump was put in place by the Globalists to bring induce economic collapse, would he have been able to bring about the record economic gains we've seen from him and his administration in just a little over a year in office? Unlikely.

President Trump has ushered in record-levels of prosperity for middle and working class Americans. This is not the work of a cut-out!

Failing to Fully Appreciate the Historical Significance of Donald Trump is its own form of Cognitive Dissonance

The idea that the Globalist Establishment is invincible was until recently not at all uncommon. But now that we understand who's been ruling us and what they represent, should we conclude that their reign of terror will last forever? Putting forth the theory that a Trump Presidency was what the Globalist Elite "wanted all along," and that Trump was likely in on the deception smells strongly of a Deep State Psy-Op that plays on the public's deep-seated belief in the eternal and immemorial invincibility of that Globalist Elite.

But do the Globalists not bleed? Are they not human? Are they infallible? They may believe themselves to be Gods, but we know they're not. They have exploitable weaknesses. They have largely brought about their defeat through their insatiable greed. Trump is just helping the process along.

Cognitive dissonance is a powerful drug. It makes otherwise-very-intelligent people goofy and incoherent in their thinking and blinds them to certain realities that they should normally see right in front of their noses."
Smith, *Zerohedge*

That statement is not only true of the Globalists, but also of Smith himself. It's he that suffers from an acute case of cognitive dissonance, for he fails to see what's right in front of his nose – namely, that Trump is a different man for different times.

This is the Second American Revolution (or a continuation of the 1st American Revolution, however you prefer to look at it). For the first time in a long time (and that could be a very long time), the Globalists are frightened! Not only are they trying to muzzle Deplorables through massive censorship campaigns, they're throwing everything and the kitchen sink at President Trump. They will continue to do all they can to derail, discredit and delegitimize him. Why? Because their very existence is at stake!

Donald Trump, while not perfect, is unlike any previous President in my lifetime. He's not a sell-out. He hates seeing Americans getting screwed over. He wants peace and prosperity for the country that aligns with the founding principles of the nation. He's not a Globalist but a Nationalist, and through understanding how the system really works, he has not allowed himself to be compromised by the Globalist Establishment.

As Alex Jones rightly continues to bellow, "We're living in historic times."

The problem is, as Jones also points out, many smart men like Smith and Icke fail to see that their own time can actually be historic! When one is so close to the change—like we are today—it tends to be difficult to recognize. For much of his adult life, Trump has been playing the long game with the American Political system. He's planning to overturn the entire New World Order project or die trying. **Trump is a System Buster.**

Bringing down Deep State is based less on physical warfare than it is on a change in thought and psychology. MAGA and the Golden Age are products of mindset. All possibilities are on the table and there for the taking.

What a time to be alive!

12 Globalism Unmasked

Our politicians have aggressively pursued a policy of Globalization, moving our jobs, our wealth and our factories to Mexico and overseas. Globalization has made the financial elite who donate to politicians very, very wealthy. I used to be one of them.

Donald Trump
June 28, 2016 Campaign Speech, Pennsylvannia

The secret to the success of Brexit and to an even larger extent that of President Trump has been the willingness to at long last call out the enemy by name: Globalists! This means Trump, the Brexiteers, Hungary, Poland, the Czech Republic and the growing number of Nationalist, Populist movements gaining momentum in Europe and throughout the world are grounded in reality.

Despite the fact that Globalists continue to gaslight the public by proclaiming there's no such thing as World Government, at the recent World Government Summit in Dubai, America was literally declared "Enemy #1!"

The situation has become so dire for them that they tell us publicly now exactly what they plan to do. George Soros does this all the time. Soros recently stated that the EU must "end populism and shut down alternative media." But...Globalism and World Government doesn't exist. Right...

Anyone with eyes to see and ears to hear realizes that clearly marked political battle lines have been drawn worldwide. These lines no longer have anything to do with Left or Right, and increasingly little to do with being Liberal or Conservative. Either you are a Globalist or an Anti-Globalist. Deplorables are fiercely Anti-Globalist.

Who are the Globalists? Best way to know is not to look at their race, class, nationality, religion or political affiliation, but instead examine what they do!

Globalists typically believe in the need for world government, open borders, multi-lateral trade deals, political correctness, identity politics, cultural Marxism, pop culture, economic feudalism, monopoly, regime change, randomness, coincidence, atheism, intolerance for ideological diversity, nepotism and centralization.

Anti-Globalists tend to believe in national sovereignty, primacy of truth, clearly defined borders, respect and adherence to the Law of the Land, local customs, tradition, constitutional law, free speech, debate, the right to bear arms, fair trade, innovation, creativity, meritocracy, intelligent design, God and decentralization.

What a contrast!

In the recent past, to even identify the Establishment as "Globalist" was to smear yourself as a conspiracy theorist. Case in point: Alex Jones and *Infowars*. For years, even when *Infowars* enjoyed some grassroots popularity, it was considered to be comprised of a bunch of conspiratorial kooks. Now, along with *Drudge, Breitbart, Prison Planet Cernovich Media, Vox Popoli* and a continuously growing number of other outlets, *Infowars* attracts more followers than such stalwart media groups as *CNN, MSNBC, CBS,* and *ABC* combined! How did that happen?

Infowars does real research and real journalism. Its team and many who work with them actually engage in honest, fact-gathering, fact-communicating journalism. When the Legacy Media attempted to label now-respected "alternative" media as "Fake News," that strategy backfired, since an increasing number of media consumers understand that it's the big fossilized media outlets that are the main propagators of fake news. MSM pissed in the wind and soiled themselves.

Jones and his team have not only tasked themselves with the daily monitoring and tracking of Globalist activities, but also take the time to read the Globalists' own white papers that openly call for World Government. If the Globalists are hiding, increasingly it's in plain sight. Therefore, for anyone now entering the political arena, to deny the existence of Globalism, which is actually one of the two most powerful forces in world politics today (and has been growing in power for at least 250 years), is tantamount to political suicide.

Is it any surprise then that the Democratic Party is in a state of utter chaos and disarray? With few to no exceptions, moderate and progressive Democrats alike are all on Team Globalism.

Globalist RINOs (Republicans In Name Only) and Cuckservatives (those on the Right who like to watch their own get screwed by the Left) are no better than (one could even argue they're the same as) their Globalist Democratic counterparts. When President Trump decided to hold his nose while foregoing the 3rd Party route to the White House—because he couldn't have won by doing so even if he had wanted to—and join a corrupt, elitist, largely Globalist Republican party, we all pray that this will not prove to have been a Faustian bargain.

Completely dependent upon the huge sums of corporate money required to mount a successful run for political office, the majority of Republicans are thoroughly intertwined with Globalism. Prime examples are Paul Ryan, Mitch McConnell, Lindsey Graham, and John McCain. Some even go as far as to say that McCain is actually the true leader of the Democratic Party, and after his "nay" vote on Healthcare Repeal and Replace (while for years running on that platform), it's difficult to argue otherwise!

True conservatives and libertarians like Matt Gaetz, Jim Jordan, Devin Nunes, Chuck Grassley and a handful of other congressional warriors, politicians who seemingly have not been hijacked by Globalism, are a little different, and perhaps offer a ray of hope to the possibility of reform of the Republican Party. These politicians on the Right side of a Globalist-corrupted bipartisan system typically see the traditions, culture and Law of the Land trampled upon by Globalists and their minions. As such, it's somewhat easier for politicians on the Right to cross over into anti-Globalism than it is for progressive Democrats who, saturated by cultural Marxism in the mainstream media, academia, Hollywood and Popular Culture, are actually moving further and further inside the Globalist echo chamber.

In other words, genuine conservatism can (but often times can not due to the corrupt nature of politics in Washington) become a fast track to an Anti-Globalist perspective, but Progressivism, which by its very nature is utopian, is far more disconnected from the Anti-Globalist reality.

Unfortunately for the Democrats, by failing to name the Enemy (Globalism) and articulate its agenda, the problem inherent in what they define as the enemy: "Corporations," "The 1%" and "Wall Street" persists because not only are the concepts too general and amorphous, otherwise sane Progressives fail to locate those entities within their proper Globalist context. Subsequently, their message remains hopelessly mired in irrelevant generalities that fail to connect with voters motivated not by vague fantasies but by specific realities that cause them problems in their everyday lives. To counter an enemy, you have to name him, study every detail of him, put yourself in his shoes, and learn his tricks in order to anticipate his movements and formulate a strategy to defeat him.

There's also a spiritual dimension to the problem. For atheists, reality is a random, inadvertent consequence of blind chance, but for those who believe in a Divine Creator, reality is a product of Intelligent Design.

Globalist-leaning Progressives tend to be atheistic and cannot ascribe to the idea of a Globalist agenda, because for them, life is purely random, a product of chance, and has no purpose or design. That's why for them, to be labelled as a Conspiracy Theorist is, has been, and always will be the ultimate insult. For Progressives, there is neither God nor Devil, Good nor Evil. They are blind; blind to reality; blind to the enemy; and most critically, blind to themselves.

Is it any wonder then that Progressives tend to exist within a cultic bubble and worship materialism? For them, material objects are the only things that are real. For Progressives, things are real, and ideas are dangerous phantoms. Debate is discouraged. Learning is frowned upon. Revision of perspectives is heretical. Reality then becomes merely what you in your bubble imagine it to be, and woe to those who try to tell you otherwise. "Kill the Messenger" is the Progressive's unspoken motto. This is why Globalists and their Progressive minions and dupes are losing the Culture War.

Progressives respond in the most Pavlovian way to incessant Globalist programming, and they're totally incapable of stepping outside that programming to acknowledge its existence. For them, there are no programmers, and it's "Conspiracy Theory" to claim that programmers exist.

Subjected to what they perceive as constant dissonance invariably gives rise to a strong desire to silence and censor. This is a big reason why Free Speech is constantly under attack, as well as why the Left seems entirely incapable of debating the issues.

Throughout his campaign and since taking office, President Trump has gained the support of his Deplorable constituents because he dares name the enemy when his opponents will not. He names and takes action against real threats like Radical Islamic Terror and exposes the phantom threats like Climate Change. President Trump paints a picture of reality that Deplorables know from experience to accurately reflect the truth about what's really going on in their lives. That is how elections are won today and will continue to be won in the foreseeable future. Ignorance is no longer an excuse.

Pretending the problem doesn't exist is a loser's path. Failure to describe the Globalist phenomenon in detail translates to inarticulate arguments that are certain to be drowned out by the deafening roar of reality.

Make no mistake. These truly are historic times. We are in a war against Globalism. Not with tanks and guns but with information and ideas. Politicians and political parties who acknowledge that this war is going on, who its participants actually are, and communicate that reality to their constituents are the only ones who will win votes and remain in office. The Globalist genie—who is the mortal enemy of humanity—has been identified, is out of the bottle and can no longer be stuffed back in. Ignore it at your own risk; fight it and win your freedom back.

The restoration of The Republic has begun.

13 The America First Party (A1P): Globalist-Free and Proud

I'm not offended when I hear President Donald Trump say 'America First.' I want 'America First' for the American people; I want 'Britain First' for the British people and I want 'France First' for the French people.

Marechal Le Pen
CPAC, Washington D.C., February 21, 2018

Isn't it high time we Deplorables had a party of our own?

In order to gain a foothold in Washington and establish a beach-head for national sovereignty, President Trump understood that to get elected, he had no choice but to hold his nose and align himself with the lesser of two evils: the largely cucked, Globalist Republican party.

Clearly the Democratic and Republican Parties are both rotting Globalist corpses. The only difference between the two is that the former is decomposing quicker than the latter. And since both Republicans and Democrats are funded by Globalists, their predominant ideology and purpose will always be Globalist. The old binary paradigms of Right vs Left, and Liberal vs Conservative are dead. What really matters today and in the future is whether your party is Pro-Globalist or Anti-Globalist.

With Trump in office, 63+ million Deplorables can begin the timely and necessary task of creating our own MAGA-compatible, Globalist-free third party that not only shares much in content and spirit with that of the Founding Fathers but is capable of carrying the America First and MAGA principles into the near and possibly even distant future.

Deplorables are mortally opposed to:
- World Government
- Open Borders
- Multilateral Trade Deals
- Political Correctness
- Identity Politics
- Cultural Marxism
- Pop Culture
- Economic Feudalism
- Federal Income Tax
- Fiat Currency
- Central Banking Control
- Monopoly
- Regime Change
- Unlimited Corporate Campaign Financing
- Mainstream media Monopoly
- Belief that all events are random and coincidental
- Moral Relativism
- Atheism
- Intolerance for Ideological Diversity
- Unfettered Artificial Intelligence
- Genetic Modification
- Climate Change
- Geoengineering
- Forced Vaccinations
- Nepotism
- Secrecy
- Centralization
- Pedophilia
- Media and Deep State Censorship of Free Speech and truth-based journalism.

At the core of President Trump's MAGA promise is the idea, America First (A1). At first glance, one might think the message is hyper-nationalist, as in "America is the best and all other countries are a distant second." That would be a gross misunderstanding. The fact is, it's a necessary antidote to the idea that long prevailed under Globalism, namely that we must think of the world first and America a distant second. In such a scenario, America becomes little more than an after-thought and an impediment to a World-First ideology.

According to America First, we Americans consider our national interest first. And when more countries start to consider their own interests rather than Globalist interests (which are monopolist interests) first, each of those countries benefits! America First = 1776 Worldwide.

That's why I am hereby calling for the immediate establishment of the America First Party (A1P).

Today it's America First (A1P). Tomorrow it's England First (E1P). Then Germany First (G1P), Russia First (R1P), Mexico First (M1P), Japan First (J1P), China First (C1P), etc.; all free, sovereign nations looking after the interests of their own citizens first with each sovereign nation capable of making mutually beneficial bilateral deals with each other.

The working <u>A1P Platform</u> includes but is not limited to the following principles:

- God
- National Sovereignty
- Clearly-defined borders
- Extreme vetting of all expatriates for terrorist ties
- A genuine pledge of allegiance to the Law of the Land
- Free Speech
- Debate
- The Right to Bear Arms
- Fair Trade
- Bilateral Trade Deals
- Promotion of Economic Competition
- No Federal Income Tax
- Non-participation in the United Nations
- Campaign Finance Reform
- Interest-Free Printing of US Dollars (not Federal Reserve Notes) by US Treasury overseen by Congress
- Abolition of the Federal Reserve System
- Extreme Vetting of all Non-Governmental Organizations (NGOs)
- Technological Innovation used to serve Humanity
- Creativity
- Renaissance Culture
- Meritocracy
- Intelligent Design
- Fair Play for Truth-based Journalism
- Energy Independence
- Transparency
- Decentralization

My hope is that within the next 4-8 years of Trump's presidency, a Globalist-free A1P can become established at every level of American political life: town, city, county, state and federal.

While it's unlikely that the two major parties will ever reform themselves, it *is* possible that Deplorable candidates will run for office either as Democrats or Republicans and replace the dead Establishment weight. But even if that happens, a viable third party that can win 5-10% of the vote in any given election can swing that election for the more Deplorable candidate running in the major party, and that's a good thing!

Meanwhile, it's quite possible that A1P's sovereign affiliates in other countries will also have made great headway, as bridges of genuine friendship are built among nations, and we at long last enter—free from parasitical Globalist tyranny—a new Golden Age.

#A1PGlobalistFree

14 Putin, Trump & Deplorables' Uncommon Common Sense

Things will work out fine between the U.S.A. and Russia. At the right time everyone will come to their senses & there will be lasting peace!

DonaldTrump
Twitter, April 13, 2016

Deep State Mainstream media (DSMSM) and Public Education continue to present reality in terms of opposing pairs: A-B. Leaving out the critical third element, "C," eliminates from the equation consciousness, perspective and synthesis, which is what we need to evolve as individuals and transform societies from Globalist Dystopias into thriving Republics.

While A-B is the reactive, binary, Pavlovian model for society favored by Globalists, the A-B-C paradigm is indicative of the Common-Sense modality advocated by Deplorables.

Rare among today's leaders, Vladimir Putin and Donald Trump clearly favor an ABC approach to governance that seeks to promote unity, social cohesion and commonality of purpose on a national and international scale.

Globalism's typical answer to the problem of populations lacking in common sense is to oppress them into total submission and serfdom, with increased submission leading to an ever more constrictive cycle of dominance, oppression and abuse. Operationally, the Globalists accomplish their goals by locking humanity into a system characterized by dualism, stimulus-response programming, disinformation, mind control, deviancy, isolation, separation, competition, narcissism and egotism.

Common Sense is part of humanity's spiritual endowment and is similar to the Greek idea of knowledge or *nous*, which is the divine spark or knowledge within that is shared or common to all. And that's why the Globalists hate and fear a renaissance of common sense!

President Putin's uncommon common sense has driven his realism-based domestic and foreign policy. President Trump, a largely non-ideological, successful businessman and resultist, shares these traits with President Putin. This not only makes the two men natural allies, but at least on a philosophical level, implacable foes of Globalist hegemony. Both men are common sense pragmatists who as a general rule reject ideology for strategies that produce results.

Besides the fact that it's bad for NATO business, the Globalist Deep State recognizes that Trump and Putin share this intelligent lack of ideology that is anathema to Globalist machinations. The Globalists are therefore desperate to prevent this alliance between two great patriots of two great nations from taking place. It's no coincidence then that Presidents Trump and Putin are the two most vilified men in the mainstream press, and the number of hysterical Fake News stories about their nefarious complicity are legion.

While Russophobia functions as DSMSM's new McCarthyism, a large segment of the awakened Deplorable media sees value in forging a better understanding of

Vladimir Putin and his proven success against Globalism. Just look at how he put his money where mouth was in Syria. And look at how he kicked George Soros out of Russia. We American Deplorables want to do the same with Soros here!

There's good reason why Putin has enjoyed sky-high approval ratings throughout his tenure. His emphasis on the importance of dialogue and discourse stands in stark contrast to the Globalist Left's assault on free speech and inability to engage anti-Globalists in any form of meaningful dialogue. Russia knows from bitter experience how stiflingly oppressive Marxist ideology can be, and how the Oligarchy that thrives in that swamp can utterly destroy a nation.

Compliance with Globalist *diktat* is ensured by its ability to provide endless streams of mindless distractions and short-term pleasures quick as one can purchase them on credit. But clearly this course of action makes no sense; it's fatally flawed and ultimately self-destructive. Why choose isolated, short-term pleasures over long-term fulfillment? True leaders like Putin and Trump who care more about the well-being of their nation and less about lining their own pockets invariably choose what's best for the nation.

Freedom is sold cheap in exchange for a handful of trinkets and beads. But as the late great George Carlin once said: "nobody seems to notice; nobody seems to care." Good luck trying to induce the Sheeple, particularly those on the Left, to step off the gerbil wheel, swallow the red pill and slide down the rabbit hole. See how that works out. People tend to cling to their illusions until it's too late.

Self-loathing is the real ideology of hate. A beautiful exception to this is the Deplorable Movement. Since we love God, we're capable of loving ourselves, our families, our pets, nature, our communities, our nation and the world. Christianity, with the exception of its radical fringes, has always been compatible with love, community, civilization and Common Sense. It should therefore come as no surprise that Christianity in Russia has, out of the ashes of nearly 80 years of horrifically oppressive, genocidal Bolshevism ,risen higher than ever before in Russian history.

Those lacking common sense are unable to step outside his or her bubble. The inability to love thy neighbor, to empathize, *i.e.* to put oneself in the shoes of another keeps the Pavlovians strapped to their egotistical, narcissistic, identitarian beds. And they won't snap out of it until their heads (often literally) are in the toilet.

Perhaps this is why those cast in the role of Controllers – along with their robotic minions – are as nasty and brutish as they are, since it falls on them to rouse the masses in the only way so many seem to understand: by shoving their faces deep down into the toilet bowl of an unexamined life. Spend enough time down there, and you may finally see that all your dreams of wealth, success and material gain have just been so much meaningless crap.

While we in America, a young country, have been relatively spared, Russian history is chock-full of examples of rude awakenings, and it therefore should not be so surprising that today's Russian population seems to be relatively more awake than those still snoozing in the West.

Vladimir Putin has not only been instrumental in helping Russia transition out of many decades of catastrophic, Bolshevist rule, but also from the cruel and heartless rape of the Russian economy by the Globalist-sponsored Oligarchs that followed in the 1990s—all the while standing tall against a growing Muslim population and the encroachment of Radical Islam.

A true alliance between Russia and the United States—which is everything the Deep State and its international attack dog, NATO, is desperate to prevent—is the lynchpin to peace and prosperity not only in our two nations but worldwide.

As it's presented today, the Globalist Con's "reality" is designed to stroke the mass ego consciousness with just enough happy endings to keep the System machine humming, while its occasionally unruly parts are alternately motivated, sedated and restrained.

The Great Awakening that many feel today, and it is palpable, is growing. Evidence? 63+ million Common Sense Deplorables voted for President Trump, and Russia, though not perfect, has become a great, emphatically Christian, Common Sense nation again.

Deplorables who are frustrated and at odds with Globalist domination strategies should find solace in the fact that the dream of a New World Order, must, according to its unnatural and unsustainable underlying principles, inevitably collapse under the weight of its excessive greed. The Moneychangers' tables will be overturned.

Russian-American alliance is inevitable and will happen sooner than people think. And for Globalists, that means Game Over Deep State. You've been outlanked.

The fundamental question of our time is whether the West has the will to survive. Do we have the confidence in our values to defend them at any cost? Do we have enough respect for our citizens to protect our borders? Do we have the desire and the courage to preserve our civilization in the face of those who would subvert and destroy it?

                    Donald Trump, Warsaw Speech, June 6, 2017

III

In Defense of The West

15 Germany: Ground Zero for Globalist Defeat and Nationalist Revival

From: orca100@upcmail.nl
To: podesta@law.georgetown.edu
Date: 2016-02-21 00:51

The only good to come out of Europe's destruction is the total demasqué of the Multikulti-Schweinerei—to use a bit of Führerbunker logic. Thankfully, the demise of Germany and its vassal states may well spell the end of the Multikulti-Junkerklasse, which has misruled Germany for decades now, deceiving Germany's proles and peasants 24/7 from cradle to grave in every nook and cranny of German society à la the GDR and also throttling the life out of anyone suicidal enough to speak out and tell it like it is.

Wikileaks.org/podesta-emails/emailid/40193

Whoever fights monsters should see to it that in the process he does not become a monster.
Friedrich Nietzsche

Success tends to discourage introspection, and in Germany's case, its post-WW II economic prosperity (compared to the rest of Europe), combined with incessant propaganda efforts aimed at re-educating Germans about their own history have led to it being on the brink of implosion today.

As Europe's largest economy and poster child of the EU,

Germany would seem to have the most to lose if the EU were to break up. Nevertheless, while those watching from afar are shocked to see Germany overrun by largely hostile Islamic men, Angela Merkel, despite strong gains (13%) by the Anti-Immigration (AfD) party, still won the country's election, *albeit* by the smallest majority of her tenure with only 33% of the vote. How, despite such a clearly disastrous immigration policy did Merkel still manage to get re-elected?

For one thing, the vast majority of the one million immigrants brought into the country over the past two years voted Merkel. So, there's that...but in my opinion, a major factor that helps explain why so many Germans continue to vote against their own interests, is that they have been systematically programmed to misunderstand their their own history.

No one can dispute the fact that Hitler was a horrible person. In this chapter my focus is on Hitler's military strategy, particularly in terms of the war against the Bolsheviks.

Unlike the popular idea that the Nazis were Far RIGHT, the socialism of the Nazis, the National SOCIALIST party, was, like its name, Far LEFT. Yet it wasn't as Far Left as the Russian Communists. Still, you might assume that would make the Nazis and Communists friends. They weren't. The Soviets had the bigger war machine.

I believe Hitler knew Stalin could crush his army through sheer numbers, weapons manufacturing and energy resources (oil), so he'd need to *blitzkrieg* them. Stalin however was thinking the same thing. He likely figured that Hitler would not be foolish enough to attack with weaker forces, but he was also likely confident he could overwhelm German forces in an assault on Europe. Was really a pretty desperate situation for the Germans.

While both countries had signed a long-term non-aggression pact, both were angling for the inevitable war to come.

In the end, by attacking Soviet forces aligned in an offensive position, which made the Soviet planes and tanks sitting ducks for the German air force, Germany was able to seize the advantage. Although the Germans would eventually lose at Stalingrad, and like Napoleon a little over a century earlier get decimated by the Russian winter, few can argue that this didn't buy time for the allies to be in a better position at the end of the war to at least save Western Europe from falling under the Iron Curtain.

A little background: Germany suffered mightily under the burden of undeserved Versailles Treaty reparations, and in its weakened state very nearly succumbed to the rampant spread of Communism. During the 1930s, while Hitler was overseeing a Globalist-funded revival of the German economy and a strengthening of its military, Stalin was very quietly (in terms of the Western press) amassing a European invasion force. Stalin was a hair late in pulling the trigger. If instead he had been a hair early, the history of post-war Europe would likely have turned out quite differently.

Bolshevism/Communism's stated goal of global revolution was and always has been little more than a cover for the Globalist agenda for a New World Order. The same Globalist bankers (who also funded the Nazis) and assorted Oligarchs funded the Communists and were hell-bent on using the Soviet Golem as a lethal weapon against the various national republics of Europe. Unlike the Soviets with their stated goal of world revolution, Hitler, at least at the beginning of the war, appeared more concerned with consolidating regional rather than global power, and thus limited his ambitions to territory that had up until very recently been German with large German populations, such as in Silesia and the Sudetenland.

Nazism was also a movement beneficial to the aims of the New World Order, but not on the same scale as Marxist/Bolshevist. Domination of academia and media by cultural Marxist ideology only seems to allow for the diversity of populations, *i.e.* "Multiculturalism," without allowing for the necessary diversity of ideas. Binary understandings of history inhibit both intellectual growth as well as empathy for others.

Europe is still under attack. But rather than the Soviet Army serving as the tip of the spear, in their place we have the Globalist-funded, unelected stalking horse of the European Union with its migrant Jihadi soldiers pouring in, as the Globalists and their 1.5 billion strong (and rapidly growing) Muslim proxies aim to finish the job that the Bolsheviks started. Meanwhile, no one except those who dare risk condemnation, incarceration and death dare say a word about it! Sad as this state of affairs is, there are glimmers of hope:

Vladimir Putin's anti-Soros Russia, anti-Soros border-protection policies in Poland, Hungary and the Czech Republic, Iceland's expulsion of their criminal Banking Elite, Brexit, the 2016 US election, the rolling back of ISIS in Syria and Iraq; these are all positive developments that are throwing a spanner into the works of the Globalist agenda. More and more national patriots around the world are joining the fight—be it armed with information or physical weapons—against Globalist shills, paid thugs and mercenaries. Theirs is an ideology of greed, destrution and censorship, which at the height of its devastating power cannot by its unnatural state of being avoid collapsing in upon itself.

Germany needs to return to its pre-Nazi origins, understand its fascist roots both for what they really were and were not, cease the stifling of free speech, reverse the devastating effects of the migrant crisis, reject multiculturalism as a false ideology designed to destroy German culture, and reclaim its historical, centuries-long leadership position as Champions of the West.

16 French Cheese Smells Bad but Tastes Good!

The French love to elect a new government providing it's the same as the old one.
Honore de Balzac

While "Far Right" candidate Marine Le Pen won 35% of the Runoff vote, finishing a solid second overall, Emmanuel Macron, the faux outsider and former Rothschild banker won easily. Huge win for the Globalists. Unfortunately for the French, they'll likely have to watch their quality of life deteriorate even further before they're compelled to make a change with their vote.

On an encouraging note, Le Pen garnered 44% of the Youth Vote. Macron enjoyed the most support from the 65 and over crowd: 80% voted Encore Marche (Emmanuel Macron, En Marche, E M, get it...not too narcissistic...), while Le Pen only managed to win 10% of the Parisian vote. Macron is popular with Seniors, urban cosmopolitan types, the wealthy, the very wealthy, the poor and the immigrants. Le Pen's support came from rural France and youth 18-24. While they may not have won the highest office of the land, I like the French Nationalists' chances for the future.

While Socialism in Europe may be fool's gold, up until the advent of the Migrant crisis, it's provided a viable safety net for the majority of its citizens. This seems to be especially true of French seniors who reportedly were extremely wary of Le Pen's proposal to leave the Euro and return to the French Franc. In their minds, a Le Pen win would have meant an unacceptable level of uncertainty in terms of the value of their pensions. But these fears are not limited to French seniors; it's demographically widespread.

Just as in his time, the great French novelist, Honore de Balzac called our attention to the French electorate's perennial, paradoxical desire for change without change, today's French voters chose the same Globalist-sponsored socialist actors devoted to the decade-by-decade hollowing out of French tradition and culture. With the country now over 20% Muslim and a majority of citizens—as demonstrated by the Election results—preferring to identify themselves more as European than French, this cultural double-whammy is killing the nation formerly known as France.

Marine Le Pen, while extremely smart and charismatic, has a major problem; her last name is Le Pen. She simply cannot escape the damaging association with her father, a man rightly or wrongly associated with Neo-Nazism. This is highly unfortunate, since Marine appears to have every attribute necessary for effective leadership. The problem then is not Le Pen's agenda, it's the permanently tainted Le Pen brand.

What I would suggest is Le Pen promote a promising up-and-comer who adheres to her platform but does not share her name. That I believe is the likely path to victory within the next 10 years. That's a long time given the current socio-cultural death spiral. The country may not survive another ten years, but that's where France is at.

With power more centralized and flowing from the top

down, the Globalists in France (and Germany) have been able to successfully limit the potentially devastating effect of social media upon Establishment narratives to a greater degree than what we see in the US. Could disarming the public have something to do with it? Just wondering...

It's still possible for the French Establishment to be attacked and undermined via social media. Le Pen would therefore be best served to focus like a laser beam on the French Populist movement's crafting of effective social media and citizen journalism platforms. This will be needed for the movement to make greater gains in the Free Speech/Political Correctness trenches, as well as in Academia. With both of these institutions, Media and Academia, having longstanding cultural Marxist roots, it'll be tough sledding for the Nationalists. Nevertheless, the France First Movement needs to plow forward. Even if progress remains modest, I expect it to remain steady.

This of course begs the question: where is the French Alex Jones? The French Paul Joseph Watson or the French Stefan Molyneux? Where is the French Cernovich? We American Deplorables are, in terms of our effective rebels, ahead of the curve. Other freedom-loving nations wishing to preserve their sovereignty and culture would be wise to follow our lead when it comes to circumventing MSM and Deep State via social media. But how is that even possible without functioning First (Free Speech) and Second (the Right to Bear Arms) Constitutional Amendments like we have in the United States?

From that constitutional foundation, freedom depends on building, maintaining and expanding anti-Globalist platforms. Even President Trump, despite all his campaign success with Twitter, has barely scratched the surface of social media's power to push his agenda forward with greater reach, rapidity and impact. At the very least POTUS should be having a "Fireside Chat" weekly podcast, and a lot more tweeting—both his own tweets as well as a condensed Executive Branch "Drudge Report" comprised of links to articles that promote the Trump Administration agenda.

Calling out Deep State Mainstream media (DSMSM) as "Fake News" and skewering them with memes is funny, effective and true, but in the long run, the President needs to take action to break up the DSMSM monopoly and allow more independent and alternative media voices to be heard. We need him to be more vocal about this. The pace of this change must pick up if we want to defeat the Fake News and re-establish the true purpose of the Fourth Estate: which traditionally has been adherence to Truth.

I can scarcely think of anything nobler and more relevant to the fight against Globalism than engaging in the Culture War and contributing to the battle over First Amendment freedom of speech, which, make no mistake, is under massive attack.

Suppression of Free Speech was fundamental to the Globalist victory in France. The Media War is fought in the trenches. Win there, and more anti-Globalists will win elections. This is currently more difficult in Western Europe than in the United States due to the fact that Hate Crime legislation is enforced to a much greater degree in Europe. When Muslims commit terrorist acts in Europe, it's unlawful to name them as Muslims, and the mainstream media there won't report the perpetrator's ethnicity either. Post the truth on Facebook or Twitter in Europe and you can be arrested and jailed. It's that bad!

When it comes to free market populism, we in the States are a click ahead of the French. Their time (along with the Dutch, Austrians, Swedes and eventually even the Germans) will come, and when it does, just as the Democrats are currently ruined here, the French Left will similarly find itself in a state of disarray. Why? Globalism equals emptiness. There's nothing to nourish the soul of the people, and socialism is an ideological dead end. History has proven that fact over and over and over again.

It's one of life's great ironies that the longer a cheese ages the more it stinks but the better it tastes. When a true Populist does take the prize in France—and I predict that will happen within the next 5-10 years—I plan to crack open a very expensive bottle of French wine, slice up some of the most pungent Camembert I can find, and savor every glorious mouthful.

Vive la France!

17 Dutch Deplorablization: Too Little Too Late?

Gather information, get the whole story, and don't jump to conclusions or judge.
Donald Trump
Trump 101: The Way to Success

If there's one thing I learned from the disappointing yet silver-lined Dutch Presidential elections, it's that the Dutch are not us. And by us, I mean Deplorables.

Courtesy of *Wikipedia*, note these general observations about Dutch character:

- Ostentatious behavior is to be avoided.
- Accumulating money is fine, but public spending of large amounts of money is considered something of a vice and associated with being a show-off.
- A high lifestyle is considered wasteful by most people and sometimes met with suspicion.
- Dutch egalitarianism is the idea that people are equal, especially from a moral point of view, and accordingly, causes the somewhat ambiguous stance the Dutch have towards hierarchy and status.

Does it sound to you like the Dutch would be huge Donald Trump fans?...hmmm...

Is Geert Wilders Trump? No, but like it or not, he and other European Populists will be associated with him.

President Trump is a brash and bold individual. He's rich. Very rich. He's flashy. He's bold. He doesn't really fit the profile for a more consensus-driven society like the Dutch have. Same likely goes for many other Continental Europeans and Scandinavians with long-running Social Welfare states. The majority of Europeans long-insulated by their Socialist safety nets, collectivist mindset and consensus-driven societies seem to have developed a distaste for rugged American individualism. Better to get along than stand out. I get it.

By the way, you know who admires rugged individualism? The Russians. That's a big reason why our alliance makes so much sense, and why together, Russia and the US are best-equipped to turn back the clocks on the Islamic 5th column advance into Europe and America. But I digress.

One thing that the Dutch are noted for which is similar to us Deplorables is their appreciation of straight talk. President Trump is as direct and plain-spoken as they come. If he continues to deliver on his campaign promises, this will no doubt go a long way towards creating greater numbers of DeploraDutch. But for a Trumpian candidate like Wilders to one day take home all the marbles in Holland, there are perhaps even more cultural and historical hurdles to clear than Trump had in America.

Though we are getting closer, we need to temper expectations when it comes to thinking the Populist candidate is going to win every election in Europe. That said, Europeans have become increasingly red-pilled to the parasitical nature of Globalism. More and more they resent having no say over the decisions of the unelected EU bureaucracy in Brussels, and have begun to recognize that the EU migration policy being forced upon them is truly a disastrous Trojan Horse.

To us diehard Deplorables, if Europe is in even more dire straits in its fight against Globalism than we are, how could their Populist candidates not be winning in a landslide every time?

Let's examine some recent history that may help explain the divide. 20th Century Europe can be divided into two periods:

- WW I and WW II with the battle between forces of Decentralization (Nationalism) and Centralization (Globalism)
- Post-WW II prosperity via the Social Welfare State.

During the war years, the New World Order favored the Bolshevist monopoly/oligarchy model but could in theory also accept Fascism because it led to essentially the same monopolistic/oligarchic model.

There was however a third way that was being actively suppressed. This was the American Model: a Jacksonian Democratic, sovereign, decentralized system that from a national perspective had worked so well during different phases of American history, particularly when there was no active fiat currency-issuing central bank. This economic model, largely borrowed from us, had also been wildly successful beginning in the second half of the 19th Century in Germany. Not surprisingly, this was one of the driving factors behind the NWO's maniacal attempt to destroy Germany during World War I. The decentralized American System could not be allowed by the Globalists to take root in Europe since it was anathema to both Marxism and Fascism (though in reality, what we labelled as "Fascism" in Germany was really another, slightly less totalitarian form of Socialism).

Holland is a relatively small country of 17 million people. It does not have a large army. It needs to go along to get along. The level of cultural Marxist propaganda that a Post-War rebuilding Europe received was initially quite mild. Citizens were well-taken care of by the State in the form of healthcare benefits, pensions and virtually free higher education. Taxes were high, and it was difficult for entrepreneurs to successfully cut through the abundance of red tape, but life was relatively peaceful and secure. There existed a robust middle class. Perhaps it was difficult for anyone to aspire beyond middle class status, but overall, European citizens seemed to be ok with that. Certainly it was preferable to war, but it was more than that. The social contract between citizen and government was seemingly working to the benefit of both.

In the meantime, as security and the general welfare was increasing every decade in Post-War Europe, quality of life was slowly but steadily decreasing in the United States. An endless series of foreign wars, inflation, drugs, crime, poverty and

> *Equality may perhaps be a right, but no power on earth can ever turn it into a fact.*
> Honore de Balzac

a steady erosion of middle class prosperity naturally led Europeans to think that their Social Welfare System (which was really Marxism-lite), was superior to our failing, more decentralized Jacksonian American Economic system. And who could really blame them for thinking that?

Americans were heavily programmed to see the enemy as foreign, when really it was domestic. Massive expansion of the Deep State corporatist combine, in conjunction with a disastrous debt-based, fraudulent Federal

Reserve system was stifling American freedom and strangling prosperity. American Tories (who had never really been defeated during the American Revolution, but had simply gone underground, biding their time until conditions became more favorable again) were in control. We had been duped! But rather than do anything about it, we retreated into our personal bubbles and sucked our thumbs. We didn't want to take responsibility for how screwed up everything really was. We just wanted to roll over and go back to sleep!

Enter the 21st Century and 911. The Globalist-whipped American Imperial horse goes into hyper-drive destabilizing the Middle East while stirring up an Islamic hornet's nest. Meanwhile the EU begins to flex its autocratic muscles, taking over more and more national decisions for its members, as it busts open European borders and allows a huge influx of largely incompatible, military-aged Muslim men into Europe in order to rape, pillage and dominate a disarmed public. Post-WW II 20th Century European peace and prosperity start to appear to the average European to be a distant memory. Complain about it, and the PC thought police make sure you shut the hell up. It begins to dawn on many Europeans that perhaps they too have been duped!

Unfortunately for the Dutch and other European nations reluctant to break out of the Nanny State mentality, times have changed. Your social welfare states *by design* were just temporary stepping stones along the road to the Sovietization of Europe. That's why massive numbers of ideologically incompatible Muslims are being allowed to bully and cuck you into submission. Have you had enough?

I know, I know. You feel yourselves too charitable to not help those you seem to feel are in need, but while doing so turn a blind eye to how your centuries-old traditions are being eradicated and your women and children abused. To protest would be considered racist, intolerant, xenophobic. Thought Police are quick to pounce. Where is the European version of Alex Jones? Where is the Dutch, German and Swedish versions of Tommy Robinson? Free Speech has been suppressed and there's not enough of an outcry about it.

Too many Dutchmen and Dutchwomen are afraid to speak out and are oversensitive to being considered social outcasts. That's why Dutch Prime Minister Martin Rutte can get away with describing Wilders' authentic political movement as "the wrong kind of Populism," and still get elected!

There is no wrong kind of Populism, Martin! The voice of The People is the voice of The People. Deplorable though it may sound to you, sir, the government exists to serve the people; not the other way around! Freedom-loving European Populists cheered after Brexit and clapped after Trump, but as Wilders' distant second-place finish suggests, don't expect the Dutch to be fully on-board quite yet with Trump and his fellow Populists.

Rather than cry about not winning, we should be proud that that Geert Wilders Freedom Party (NVV) gained the seats that it did in Parliament (Wilders' NVV is now the second-largest party in Holland), and Prime Minister Rutte's ruling Party for Freedom and Democracy (VVD) lost its greatest number of seats in many years. Suffice it to say that although we really wanted the Presidency, substantial gains were made.

Throughout the last several centuries, the Europeans who resonated with the American system, namely those who felt stifled by what they perceived to be over-interference by the European State, have already emigrated to the United States and are spread throughout the Deplorable movement.

Political Correctness in Europe runs deep—deeper than in the United States. It's both a corollary of decades of Postwar economic success, and a product of centuries-old cultural differences between our two continents. Don't forget that we're still the Wild West to many Europeans.

Europe has been set up by Globalists who never had any intention of indefinitely supporting the Social Welfare State. Though it was from the start an unsustainable project, there still exists a large number of Europeans who cannot believe that is the case, and that's a big reason why they're blinded to the destruction—all by design—being wrought upon their societies by the Islamic horde and a centralized European Politburo.

If we want our European brothers and sisters to get over the hump and onboard with full-blown Deplorablism, we and our natural allies that are showing how it's done in Hungary, Poland, the Czech Republic, and, dare I say, Russia, have to lead by example. If they really want it, they'll have it.

And they'll do it their way.

18 Up Against The Wall

I'll never be a wallflower. I'd rather build walls then cling to them.
Donald Trump
Trump 101: The Way to Success

In the late 1990s, I spent two very happy years living and working in Mexico City, and while doing so developed a real love for the country, its people and its rich culture. Mexicans are a proud bunch, and many have a complex love/hate relationship with their big northern neighbor. Keeping that in mind, we need to show respect for each other and create mutually beneficial rather than one-sided agreements. President Trump knows this.

Disagreement about The Wall has shone a light on just how spineless, corrupt and mendacious Mexico's government—and not the majority of its people—really is. Though they claim to have no interest in building walls, why then are they themselves currently erecting one of their own on their southern border with Guatemala?

Why does former Mexican President Vicente Fox attempt to insult and demean our President every chance he gets and repeatedly compare Trump to Hitler?

Why does Mexico seem to care more about assisting Drug Lords than improving the lives of its own people?

It's sad, but Mexico has no "Trump" of its own, only a bunch of traitorous, self-serving "Obamas."

And then there's the North American Free Trade Agreement (NAFTA). NAFTA was always a good deal for US corporations and the Mecican plutocracy that wished to take advantage of less expensive Mexican labor at the expense of American workers. And it hasn't been much of a bed of roses either for for Mexican citizens, as there's been an explosion of narco-terrorism since NAFTA's ratification.

The US currently has a $60 billion trade deficit with Mexico. Every year, illegal Mexican migrants in the US remit billions of dollars out of the US economy back to their families in Mexico. All the while, these illegal migrants enjoy the same benefits as US citizens and legal immigrants, often without paying taxes and/or illegally participating in elections. Additionally, with a porous rather than strong border in place, the narcotics business flourishes. Innocents, particularly in Mexico, are caught in the crossfire, and international banks rake in huge profits laundering drug money. Multinationals and Drug cartels benefitted from NAFTA, but neither ordinary Mexicans nor ordinary Americans have seen any real improvement to their quality of life. Both have been victimized.

Former President Vicente Fox, an outspoken Trump critic said, "We refuse to pay for any fucking wall!" Despite his populist rhetoric, Fox clearly serves the organized crime cartel, primarily the narcotics industy in their quest to perpetuate the corrupt *status quo*. These sleazy, racist politicians have never had any interest in creating prosperity for the average Mexican.

Trump has the support of the majority of the American people to build The Wall and whether Mexico pays for it or not, one way or another, Mexico will end up paying for a good portion if not the entire expense as the trade imbalance and immigration issues are rectified. Trump was smart enough during the campaign to realize that even though his initial offer was at the extreme end of the toughness spectrum, his long game was to reset the entire Globalist-orchestrated, one-sided relationship with Mexico, which in the end will create more prosperity and freedom in both countries.

President Trump, a master deal-maker, knows full well that a good deal is good for both sides. We're both proud countries. We both need The Wall to protect the border when it comes to illegal immigration, drug-running, money laundering and international terrorism, including Radical Islamic Terrorism.

As much as the Globalists would like to keep us at each other's throats, Trump – as well as most Americans and most Mexicans—understand that strong borders and policies that benefit working people in both countries (rather than Multinationals and drug cartels) will create peace, prosperity and better long-term relations. Anything less, and we're selling ourselves short.

#UpAgainstTheWall

Postscript: President Trump ordered the National Guard deployed to the southern border. These troops will likely remain until wall construction is complete.

19 De-Golemizing Globalist Israel

There's a strange thing with Jews and Christians where there's this snobby disdain for arrogance. They see Trump as arrogant. They don't like Trump here [in Israel]. We should all change and become more arrogant and more proud. Israel should be proud of their wall because it works, and America should build its wall and be proud of it because it will work.

Gavin McInnes, Rebel Media

Many Deplorables support Israel, but Israel, while small, has an exceedingly diverse range of political and religious interests with a very powerful Deep State. I once thought that this Israeli Deep State was primarily ultra-nationalist and right wing, but based on recent behavior, it appears that this view was short-sighted. The most dangerous faction of the Israeli Deep State is coming from the Globalist Left.

The Trumpian Revolution has made it clearer than ever how most nation-states, including Israel, have for many years now both been hijacked and subsequently Golemized by Globalists, and as such have not been acting in their own best interest. Israel has often been used as a weapon by the Globalists in their incessant drive to foment national destabilization crises throughout the world for the purpose of providing their New World Order solution to that manufactured chaos.

As a member of the Nationalist elite, Trump has already begun making moves that will awaken the US from its

Globalist slumber and return it to a form that more resembles a sovereign Republic. It's a fierce, ongoing civil war with global implications, where although Trump seems for now to have the momentum, it will nevertheless be a long hard fight against a desperate, but still powerful enemy. But what about Israel?

Globalists do not want an independent, sovereign Israel, because not only do they need Israel to continue its role as Chief Shit-Stirrer, Israel stands squarely in the way of the Radical Islamic domination of the Middle East that Globalists support in order to eradicate Christianity and use the Middle East as a launch point to conquer the West. From an anatomical perspective, Israel is the sciatic nerve of the globalist body politic; tweak it and the whole world writhes in pain.

If the push for Two-State peace by the Israelis has long been disingenuous, the Globalist sponsorship of Two-State peace for the Palestinians has been equally disingenuous. Both Golemized entities—Israel and the Palestinians—were used to create strife and tension amongst their people, the region and the world, all of which has been a boon to the Globalist plan to speed up implementation of its freedom-stifling solution: The New World Order.

The fact that the Israelis have for decades oppressed the Palestinians and engaged in a process of perpetual delay in negotiations has complicated the matter, but despite this heinous policy, Israel needs to be supported in this situation against the globalist tactic of using The Two State Solution as a means for undermining Israel's security with international Islamic terrorists and/or possible takeover of the Jewish State by means of their demographic time bomb. As we've seen in Europe, just having a national population that is 5-10% Muslim can create much instability, as those populations often assert the primacy of Sharia Law over national Law of the Land.

Until recently, I actually used to advocate a One-State, power-sharing solution for Israel and the Palestinians—an "Israelistan" or "Palisrael"—but now I can neither support the One State nor the Two State solution. For the foreseeable future, Israel must remain a Judeo-Christian beachhead against the spread of Islam until the time (if ever) that Islam is able to reform itself and stop waging war on the West. While it saddens me that many moderate, peace-loving Islamic Palestinians (Christian Palestinians should be allowed to return) will not be allowed to return to their historic lands, Israel cannot risk its existence over it. In the meantime, other countries in the Middle East will have to pick up the slack and allow those Palestinians to emigrate to their countries if they wish to do so. And in the meantime, Israel should do everything in its power to make the territories where Palestinians currently live as pleasant and prosperous as possible.

> GOLEM: an artificial human being in Hebrew folklore endowed with life; automaton; blockhead.
> Merriam-Webster

While in Israel's case, nationalism can too often mean ultra-nationalism and Jewish Supremacy, at the end of the day, an aggressive nationalist Israel that still retains some imperialistic ambitions, while not to be encouraged or enabled, can hopefully become less imperialistic over time, and is still preferable to being dominated by Globalists who won't hesitate to sell Israel out to Islam, the weapon of choice used by the Globalists to destroy the West.

Prime Minister Benjamin "Bibi" Netanyahu, having recently declared war on George Soros, is being attacked by Soros-led Globalists nearly as much as President Trump, and will probably not have much choice but to step down or face prison time for corruption charges. Although it appears he's being framed, Netanyahu has been in power long enough and has worn out his welcome with the Israeli public. Time for some new blood.

Nevertheless, as long as Bibi remains in office, he needs to recognize the fact that his furtive support of radical Islamic terrorists (as he's been doing in Syria) for the sake of achieving imperialistic, Greater Israel goals was not only misguided but will boomerang against Israel if the policy continues.

Netanyahu must grasp that he and his administration have been Golemized by the Globalists in a larger game. Bibi needs to form an unbreakable bond with Presidents Trump and Putin (Russian power and interests in the Middle East cannot be ignored) to help cleanse the region of Islamic extremism, establish and implement red lines against terrorist-sponsoring Gulf States and a highly aggressive, increasingly Islamic Turkey, as well as firmly address the very real domestic economic problems (largely caused by the Globalist Debt System) that have eroded quality of life for the Israeli working class.

Also necessary is a less paranoiac approach to its treatment of Iran, the dysfunction of which seems to stem from what the writer Gilad Atzmon might likely describe as *Pre*-Traumatic Stress Disorder (PTSD), a very Jewish syndrome where you obsessively fear what *might* happen rather than what's *actually* happening. If Russia, a Christian nation, can form a functional alliance with Shia Iran, why can't the United States and Israel do the same? I realize we need reform of the Mullah system to take place in Iran, but at some point we need to recalibrate the overwhelming use of sticks to carrots when it comes to relations with Iran. President Trump's support for the anti-Hijab activists in Iran was a step in the right direction. Continue condemning Iranian leadership, but try to nudge it towards granting more freedoms for its youth-heavy, largely America-friendly population that feels oppressed by the Mullahs.

We're well aware that former President Obama made a terrible deal with Iran, and President Trump needs to reset the table for tough negotiations with Iran, but for the Israeli Deep State, Iran is to Israel as Russia is to the United States. Both Deep States must have enemies to justify military expenditures and surveillance, no matter how manufactured that enemy might be. States need to deal with States as rational actors and separate the State wheat from Deep State chaff.

By abandoning the Greater Israel project for the Middle East, which tends to dovetail with the Globalist aim of breaking up secular nation states (because prosperous nation states are far more difficult to control and Golemize than failed or failing debtor states), Israel can begin creating some badly-needed public relations for itself (something it sorely needs) by supporting real economic growth at home and peace with its neighbors abroad.

Israel needs to finally come to terms with the fact that it

too has long been used and abused by the Globalists. It no longer needs that relationship. The source of Israeli security is actually quite simple; it comes from promoting secularism and economic prosperity for itself and its neighbors. This peaceful solution will help isolate tyrannical, intolerant, terrorist-supporting, Globalist-backed Gulf States (as well as Israel's own Deep State) who oppress their own people and are causing ruinous instability throughout the world.

Long live national sovereignty, freedom, prosperity and cultural Renaissance worldwide!

Postscript: In a shot across the bow against the UN, the Muslim world and nearly all of its allies, the US has announced it will move its embassy from Tel Aviv to Jerusalem. I love it! This shows how strong the bond is between Israel and the US and it gives the US increased leverage in all Middle East peace negotiations. Now if only we could do something about that outta control Israeli Deep State...

20 China-US Relations: Heightened Tensions Obscuring Golden Opportunity

PLAYBOY: *How far are you willing to push adversaries?*

TRUMP: *I will demand anything I can get. When you're doing business, you take people to the brink of breaking them without having them break, to the maximum point their heads can handle—without breaking them. That's the sign of a good businessman. Somebody else would take them 15 steps beyond their breaking point.*

PLAYBOY: *What if your pushing results in losing the deal?*

TRUMP: *Then I pushed him too far. I would have made a mistake. But I don't. I push to the maximum of what he can stand and I get a better deal than he gets.*

Donald Trump Interview
Playboy, 1990

The against-all-odds election of Donald J. Trump is a game changer. Of this there is no doubt. While the domestic makeover will be nothing short of revolutionary, let's take a moment to reflect on windows of opportunity opening up in the area of foreign policy, and particularly in terms of the vital relationship between China and the United States. First however, some personal background and context:

Although I studied Chinese in the 1980s and lived and worked in Taiwan in the 1990s, it's only been recently that I grasped the idea that there had been a definitive role created for the People's Republic of China (PRC) in the Globalist New World Order. The reason is unsurprising.

In the 1990s, prior to the true Age of Information, claims of NWO & Illuminati control were considered quack theories to which no "informed" or "educated" person could subscribe. Though unaware of the fact, growing up in the seemingly benign and disconnected northern New Jersey suburbs of the 1970s and 1980s, like most Americans of my generation, I was weaned on a steady diet of cultural Marxism which produced an unconscious bias for the Left and against the Right. I was therefore cynical about America, finding a lot more reasons to criticize than praise it. That America was a racist, bigoted, homophobic aggressor nation was a given. I internalized all of it and left it largely unquestioned.

A word on cultural Marxism. While one can start with the post-WW II arrival of the Frankfurt School "luminaries" into the United States, and say they were its progenitors, it goes much deeper than that. It had sponsors. And the sponsors of cultural Marxism in the U.S. have been and continue to be the same sponsors of Globalism wherever it's reared its ugly head around the world.

"Globalism" is actually just modern nomenclature for Communism and Bolshevism. These ideological weapons are used to destroy countries and their cultures and create conditions for hostile, monopolistic takeovers of national economies in order to create a neo-feudalistic supply of obedient worker slaves. What's most astounding when one finally unravels this Con of Cons, is that it hides in plain sight, and the perpetrators don't even bother to cover their tracks. The public is simply trained not to see it. Therefore, it requires a certain level of inquisitiveness to discover its presence and begin understanding its Matrix-like deception. Now perhaps it's more understandable why, from the perspective of the New World Order, when I was younger, I was incapable of seeing through the fog of war to properly understand China's role and position at the top among nations. The election of Donald J Trump on November 9th, my birthday, brought forth the final piece of the puzzle for me in terms of China.

Ever since Nixon and Kissinger "opened China" in 1972, China has shied away from loudly proclaiming its growing world economic dominance, because it knew how tilted Globalists had made the playing field in its favor. Better to stay under the radar. But two funny things happened on the way to the forum: Putin's Russia and now Trump's America. The former has left the Globalist reservation and the second is in the process of leaving. For the Globalists, one departure was concerning, the second is sobering, but the third…that would be downright catastrophic!

No doubt I'm absolutely viewing this from a glass half full perspective. I'm taking a leap of faith. I'm using the logic that says overt repression as we see in China tends to hasten the downfall of regimes who practice it because it's so obvious to the people.

Glass half empty: the hurdles to bringing China into the fold are immense. Why? Control. No dissent is allowed and the internet is firewalled. All the while, incomes have risen dramatically, although the middle class has really not grown much. Prosperity in China is real, but it's been based on an artificially-stimulated bubble economy with its materialistic prosperity devoid of individual freedom. It's a bad deal for the public, and deep down the Chinese people know it, but without the communicative power of alternative sources of information, free speech, and a disarmed public, Chinese citizens feel themselves powerless to do anything to contradict or circumvent the massive, centralized, top-down power of the Communist Party and its leadership.

The Communist Party rules China with an iron fist and will not go quietly into the night. Despite massive protests in 1989 culminating in bloodshed at Tiananmen Square, the Communists not only solidified their rule, but doubled-down on repression against dissent. The leaders of the Communist Party have no intention of relinquishing power now—particularly when from a national perspective they're so close to becoming top dog within the globalist hierarchy. Additionally, there's a certain level of cultural baggage, an elitist, hierarchical tradition of Confucianism which tends to promote groupthink, and a hive-mind paternalism that's anathema to that of a freer, society for its citizens.

Now for the good news: the Globalists are losing! Like the ball that no matter how hard you try to keep underwater cannot by physical law remain submerged, they are losing. So now what can they do? Where can they turn? There are really only two places: China and the EU, and to a lesser extent, Turkey and Saudi Arabia.

Starting with Brexit, and smaller but significant Populist gains in France, Germany, Austria, Italy and the Netherlands (not to mention strong Sovereign Nationalism already in place in Hungary, Poland and the Czech Republic), the political tide in Europe is already turning and the political seas churning as indivudal European nations are poised to reverse globalist tyranny and return to its nationalist roots. If the EU dissolves,

European nations will resume making fair and sensible bilateral trade deals with each other, and it'll be back to a common-sense approach. I realize we're not there yet, but in its darkest hour, Europeans are being pushed to their absolute breaking point, which suggests, just as *Glasnost* in Russia and the fall of the Berlin Wall seemed to have happened suddenly and unexpectedly, in my view, major change is inevitable and will happen sooner than many think.

So that leaves China, the NWO's not-so-secret weapon, a Golem to be unleashed against the West. Here's the thing though: why would the Chinese, an eminently pragmatic people—with the US, Russia and Europe, moving, *albeit* slowly, towards forming a super-alliance based on national sovereignty, traditional culture and human freedom—allow themselves to be used by Globalists for their own isolation and destruction as they suddenly find themselves friendless? Even the corrupt, seemingly all-powerful Communist Party leadership will not be able to ignore this!

China's recent acceptance of sanctions against North Korea at the UN Security Council and its instrumental role (pointed out by Trump) in helping broker peace on the Korean peninsula is a very encouraging development. When push comes to shove, China (but not necessarily the formidable Chinese Deep State) wants trade and peace more than it wants war.

The new global reality will be a true test of how successful (or not) the level of brainwashing has been *vis a vis* the Chinese people by its leadership. Remember, in terms of access to information, the Chinese population has been largely cut off from the world by internet censorship. No wonder the NWO, via its Chinese proxies, wishes to extend these censorship practices to the West.

Economic success has likely only reinforced the illusion that the Chinese public's lack of freedom is necessary for prosperity. Can the truth-telling populist nationalism break through such a seemingly impenetrable wall of top down nationalist propaganda in China? Surely this is a tall task. Essentially what we're asking for is a soft Chinese coup along the lines of what's recently happened in Russia, the US and the UK.

While I'm not saying it will happen, if it did, I can't see how the Globalists survive the combined sovereign force of China, the US Russia and Europe. It will be the end of the Globalist Era and a new Renaissance on a global scale.

But let's not pat ourselves on the back just yet. As we're seeing in America, there's much swamp first to be drained just to get our own house in order, Nonetheless, if the Chinese leadership can get ahead of the inevitable counter-revolution by removing the internet firewall and allow a truly representative government to form and flourish, China can usher in a non-Zero Sum, win-win not only for itself, but for all sovereign nations around the world. To do so, it must recognize that its Globalist-sponsored rise to prosperity—while it did indeed illustrate the grit and determination of the Chinese people as well as some degree of visionary planning from the top—was largely a bubble economy propped up by international bankers who merely wished to use (and eventually abuse) China for its own nefarious, one-world government purposes.

Yes, China has all along been set up by the Globalists to contend with the United States as the enforcer nation of the world. I know this sounds conspiratorial, but all signs point to its veracity.

If unable to win over Chinese President Xi Jin Ping's good nature, then we should try appealing to his greed, ego and/or pragmatism. Show him, Presidents Trump and Putin (yes I'm assuming that eventually we'll have a working partnership with Russia), that working with us rather than against us makes sound business sense.

The Chinese need to once and for all reject the NWO and its agents and embrace a Pax China-Russia-America-Europe so that China—a country and civilization most renowned among nations for playing the long game—will prosper rather than suffer. By doing the right thing for China and its people, President Xi will forever be memorialized as not only a hero to China but to the world.

Postscript: China has removed term limits from its presidency. Xi Jinping is now "President for Life." On the surface, this appears regressive, but it's also an indication that the Chinese regime is desperate to find its footing and resistant to the inevitable change that's come about by virute of a weakened Globalist order. Meanwhile, following Kim Jong Un's visit to China, it's clear that President Xi has been instrumental in brokering of peace between North Korea, South Korea, and the US.

21 Kim Jong-Un to Kim Win-Win

> *The deal with North Korea is very much in the making and will be, if completed, a very good one for the World. Time and place to be determined.*
>
> Donald Trump, Twitter
March 9, 2018

Why not aim high, retire a hero and go from Kim Jong-Un to Kim Win-Win?

As the world eagerly awaits the upcoming face-to-face meeting between North Korean Dear Leader Kim Jong Un and President Trump, I could not help but try to place myself in Kim's shoes. Here's how I hope he sees the situation:

Holding on to power in a socialist hellhole is probably fun for a while, but eventually it becomes a drag, especially when compliance is typically enforced at the sharp point of a bayonet. This understandably fosters a climate rife with fear and paranoia. That must get old.

Why not give all Koreans what they really want and deserve: the freedom and prosperity that a unified and de-nuclearized Korea would bring? Unification would likely usher in greater peace and stability not only to the region, but to the world.

Obviously, this would necessitate your sooner-than-later relinquishing of power, Kim. That's the rub. But hey, start a new chapter. I'm sure you, your family and your closest associates will still have a prominent, profitable role in the post-unification society. Don't be afraid to let go! This is not a Qadaffi or Saddam Hussein situation. I have little doubt that you'll come out of this smelling like a rose.

Make the deal, Kim. Free and unify your people, and the US and South Korean leadership, despite all your crimes, will be happy to grant you and your top leadership immunity. Immunity you know you need. Don't worry. We promise we'll keep that bit on the down-low.

No doubt there are Deep State actors who don't want this to happen, including many of Kim's own generals. A divided Korea and a nuclear North Korea is a useful tool for instability and a key component of New World Order tyranny.

Fuck 'em! This is the Golden Age, and we're offering you a prominent role in a better world if you're willing to leave the past behind. We hope that your willingness to denuclearize, strong desire for unification and willingness to meet with President Trump are all signs that you will embrace the change from which you yourself and all Koreans can enormously benefit.

You know better than anyone that Socialism is a scam. It was just a convenient excuse for you and your family to maintain your monopoly on power. Too many of your people are starving and borderline mutinous. You can only hold them down for so long, and at the end of the day, is that really what you want your legacy to be: a ruthless dictator overthrown by his people or assassinated by his generals?

Why risk that possibility when you can win, be honored around the world as a great peace-maker, loved by all Koreans for a selfless act, and be considered a unifier of a nation divided far too long. Stepping down from power is not a bad exchange for what you receive in return.

South Korea has demonstrated it knows how to create prosperity. It may take some time, and the transition to a free market economy will have its share of bumps in the road, but Korean culture remains largely homogenous. Sooner rather than later, the economic gains and prosperity of the South will be shared by those in the North. An ancient culture, nation and perople that never should have been divided can finally be reunified.

It's time to be a hero, Kim. It's time to break the authoritarian chains of the past. You, President Trump and the Korean people can do this together.

In this situation, doing the right thing is a win-win.

#KimWinWin

While opposition to President Trump manifests itself through political warfare memes centered on cultural Marxist narratives, this hardly means that opposition is limited to Marxists as conventionally understood. Having become the dominant cultural meme, some benefit from it while others are captured by it; including "deep state" actors, globalists, bankers, Islamists, and establishment Republicans.

Rich Higgins, *POTUS and Political Warfare*

IV

Know Thy Enemy
Know Thy Self

22 #Syria: The Big White Lie that Succeeded Spectacularly

Knowledge requires patience; action requires courage. Put patience and courage together and you'll be a winner.

Donald Trump
Trump 101: The Way to Success

When President Trump ordered the firing of 59 Cruise Missiles at a Syrian airbase in Homs after an alleged chemical attack in the northwestern city of Idlib, it caught many by surprise.

Why did he do it? Was it worth it? Here's how I believe POTUS may have game planned this in his head:

Although McMaster tells me he's certain Assad was responsible for the chemical attack, clearly this was not the case. The Jihadi Rebels, backed by the US, Saudi and Israeli Deep State were the ones who benefitted, not Assad, and therefore Assad had no good reason to act against his own interest. He hasn't survived this long by being a moron. The Syrian Army is winning the war. Why jeopardize that by launching a chemical attack? Doing that makes no sense.

I know this with great certainty because this is not the first time the Jihadis have launched a chemical attack designed to falsely implicate Assad. It happened before in 2013 in Damascus. At that time, in order to stave off all-out war by the West against Syria, Putin cleverly helped broker a deal whereby the Syrians would remove and/or destroy all existing chemical weapons in their arsenal. The US backed off, and Assad bought more time. But it seems that he didn't get rid of all the chemical armaments.

This now puts the Russians in an awkward position. They don't wanna appear complicit in dishonoring the agreement they helped broker. So even though their client has been falsely blamed for the chemical attack, they can't object too loudly to the airbase attack because they don't want more attention drawn to the fact that they and the Syrians failed to completely honor their agreement to rid themselves of all their chemical weapons. This not only gives me leverage against Russia in Syria, but by appearing to act against Russia, I'll get the domestic Deep State with their false accusations of my being a Russian Agent off my back. Strengthening my partnership with Russia is a cornerstone of my fight against the New World Order, but it's not something I can just announce, because if I do, the Globalist Deep State will go ape shit!

What does Deep State have an absolute hard-on for? Syria. They're totally obsessed with it. I really don't have anything against Assad. In fact, he's the most qualified to hold that diverse group of people together—including my fellow-Christians—but the Israeli, Saudi and US Deep State have all been humiliated by the great success Russia, Iran, Hezbollah and the Syrian Army have had in rolling back the Jihadi Rebels.

I know that I need to get ISIS and all the other sick Jihadis out of Syria, and that's what I promised the American People I would do. It's what they expect and it's what I want. But in order to untie my hands with Russia, I need to put Regime Change back on the table. However, I will personally make it clear that Regime Change will only be achieved through political means and not via military force. Russia wants to move ahead with improving bilateral relations with the United States, and even if the Military Industrial Complex doesn't want it, I also want a real partnership with Russia.

But it would be political suicide to call for that now. It's currently in Russia's interest to broker a non-violent political deal with the Assad regime, which although it won't completely satisfy Deep State, it will buy me enough time to achieve my most important objective: MAGA.

By launching missiles during Premier Xi's visit to Mar-a-Lago, I will show strength and help my negotiation position with China. Kim Jong Un in North Korea will also receive a strong message that I won't hesitate to use overwhelming force when America is threatened.

That's some serious 5D chess right there, folks.

The bottom line is that a window of opportunity opened, and President Trump made the bold move to launch the strike that garnered huge benefits. Here's a recap of those benefits:

- It freed him from the "Russian Agent" hog-tying by Deep State. By making that move, Trump not only gave himself a much freer hand to negotiate with the Russians, he now has a lot more freedom and leverage to MAGA with his domestic agenda.
- It sent a message of strength to the North Koreans that has resulted in a greater willingness by them to negotiate than they've ever shown.
- It allowed Trump to make a huge impression on the visiting Chinese Premier Xi Ji Ping (the Chinese do love their fireworks!) that is already helping create a better relationship between the US and China.
- It sent a message of strength to Turkey, Iran and Hezbollah.
- It gave the US greater leverage in negotiating a Syria Peace Deal further down the road, which seemed to have borne fruit in Frankfort when Russia and the US were able to broker a peace deal in southern Syria.

At risk was:

- A bellicose reaction from Russia that could lead to the start of WW III
- Alienating the Deplorable Base by fudging the truth
- Getting bogged down in a larger war in Syria

While those risks were certainly legitimate, clearly President Trump felt they could be mitigated enough to justify the benefits of taking the action he did, and thus far this has largely proven to be the case.

That said, I do wish to propose an alternative course of action that President Trump could have taken while still covering himself against legitimate complaints that the chemical weapons attack was a False Flag:

If the Syrians were in fact storing chemical weapons at the Homs airbase – the target of the Tomahawk strike— why didn't Trump stick to that as pretext for the strike? Wouldn't that have achieved the same results at less of a "trust" cost with a False Flag-savvy Deplorable base who knows a hoax when it sees one? Speculating here, but perhaps President Trump figured that the horrific optics of a chemical attack were the surest way to win the widespread, emotional support of the general and not just the Deplorable public he needed in order to launch the attack that would reap him all those benefits. Tough call there.

Using the chemical attack as *causus belli* for the missile launch also would've had the added benefit of putting the ex-NSC Advisor, Globalist General McMaster on the hook if and when the hoax is ever revealed. In this way, Trump can blame McMaster (a bitter enemy of Deplorable nationalism) for shoddy intelligence and use that as a pretext to later fire him.

When the event first happened, I shaded the Trump-cheerleading pundit Bill Mitchell for not even acknowledging the possibility of the chemical weapons attack being a false flag. I simply wanted Mitchell to admit the fact that these particular ends justified these particular means. Mitchell wouldn't admit it, because he didn't want to promote the idea that Trump lied. My take however is that Trump lied, but it was worth it! Although it can be a slippery slope, sometimes specific ends do justify morally-dodgy means.

I admit that at first even I felt a bit stung by the President's flouting of the truth. It bothered me. I took it personally. Throughout the campaign and into the early days of the Trump administration, Deploraville invested much blood, sweat and tears in him. We expect him to honor his campaign promises. We expect him to fight Globalism. Despite what Bill Mitchell (and I'm a Mitchel twitter follower) says, ideology *does* matter!

For those who strongly value truth, this is a natural reaction to have, but that feeling of betrayal is temporarily obscured by The Bigger Picture. And that Bigger Picture is not whether Assad gassed his people (which he didn't; ISIS and Deep State did), but it's for President Trump to Make America Great Again.

Furthermore, Deplorables need to understand that Trump not only negotiates with his enemies, he negotiates with his base! Therefore, he expects pushback. If we only cheerlead and blindly (as Bill Mitchell urges his peeps to do) "Trust Trump," we lose the leverage necessary to hold

Trump's feet to the fire. Trump does not wish to be treated like a Messiah. He considers us equals!

Scott Adams, in one of his Periscopes, summed up the #SyriaHoax situation well when he stated that Trump was "like Bruce Lee, surrounded by enemies on all sides (US Deep State, Israeli Deep State, Saudi Deep State, Russian Deep State, Chinese Deep State, N Korea, Syria) and he had to kick and punch his way out." So true! How could President Trump MAGA while being so completely hog-tied by Deep State? He could not!

Getting up on that podium and assigning blame to Assad for killing those "beautiful babies" when our President surely knew who was really behind the attack—the US, Israeli and Saudi Deep State—had to have been tough.

And while the President did what he felt he had to do, Truth got a bit bruised in the process. Bitter medicine for Deploraville to swallow, but I still give POTUS a pass since he was in such a tight spot and the results were so impressive.

Great leaders are willing to take calculated risks, and that's exactly what President Trump did here. If Deploraville and the President share the same ends, and I believe we do, then sometimes we're just going to have to disagree on the means.

<u>Postscript</u>: Deja vu all over again. After announcing on April 4th, 2018, a six-month timeline for withdrawal of American forces from Syria, on April 13th, 2018, President Trump again ordered missile strikes against the Syrian government. According to US Secretary of Defense Mattis, the strikes were a "one-shot deal" made in retaliation for what was clearly another false flag chemical weapons attack. Just like last year, the typically never-Trump Mainstream media supported the measure, while the Deplorable Base was split. If the Big White Lie worked once, it's hard to blame the President for employing the same Machiavelllian tactic again. Stay tuned...

23 Pittsburgh not Paris

We came together around a strong agreement (The Paris Climate Accord) the world needed. We met the moment. We've shown what's possible when the world stands as one.

Barack Obama
December 12, 2015, Paris,
The Huffington Post

Oddly enough, I've never been to Pittsburgh, but I have been to Paris twice—both times in the 1990s—and each visit was nothing short of *magnifique*. Fast forward to May, 2018, and as the epicenter of both the Migrant Crisis and the biggest swindle of the age, *aka* The Paris Climate Accord, I neither wish to visit nor join.

I sincerely hope that not unlike our US Independence Day, June 1st, 2017 will mark the day that future generations of Americans will celebrate as the day the United States stood up and gave the middle finger to Globalism.

> *I am committed to keeping our air and water clean, but always remember that economic growth enhances environmental protection. Jobs matter!*
> Donald Trump, Twitter, April 2016

Besides the fact that in my opinion Global Warming is clearly a hoax engineered to create so much fear and guilt that Americans will be happy to sign their wealth and prosperity away in service of a lie, it's also been designed to line the pockets of a small group of Globalist Plutocrats like Al Gore, the Rothschilds, George Soros and their ilk at the expense of US sovereignty, treasure and jobs. This is totally unacceptable!

If the Paris Accord was really about the environment and not about bankrupting America, why, when President Trump, in his historic Rose Garden speech announcing our withdrawal from the treaty, offered the olive branch of renegotiation did France, Germany and Italy all immediately declare that the terms of the treaty were non-negotiable? What a crock! They know all too well that this is all about other countries and their monopolists making money at US taxpayer expense! President Trump and his Deplorable constituents were not born yesterday.

Globalist traitors like Emmanuel Macron, Angela Merkel, Crooked Hillary Clinton and former President Barack Obama are perfectly aware that the Paris Accord scam has nothing to do with "saving the environment" (a pseudo-scientific, nonsensical notion) and everything to do with crushing the US economy and enslaving its citizens in a feudalistic, technocratic jail cell. These Globalist jackals had been licking their chops, but now President Trump has forced them to lick their wounds. Thank you, Mr. President!

Donald J. Trump, a man who made his fortune building luxury hotels, casinos and apartments—tangible goods of exceptional quality that created value and jobs—saw the gutting of the American Middle Class and the slow, steady rot of the US economy not only as tragic—which it was—but bad for business!

Make no mistake about it. POTUS is turning the US Economic Ship of State around. Trillions have been added to the value of the stock market. Small Business numbers are hitting levels the likes of which haven't been reached in many, many years. Employment has been up every month since inauguration. We've made significant trade deals with China, Japan and Vietnam and we'll likely scrap NAFTA to create a much better, fairer deal for all three participants: the US, Mexico and Canada.

And now, within his first nine months in office, President Trump has withdrawn the US from disastrous Globalist trade deals like Trans Pacific Partnership (TPP) and the Paris Accords—both of which would have brought only blight and misery to the American worker.

Pittsburgh, not Paris.

America First, baby. *America* First!

24 #SethRich

Behind every great fortune lies a great crime.

Honore de Balzac

In case you haven't noticed, there's an elephant in the room named Seth Rich. *WikiLeaks* not only has Julian Assange, a man whose sterling credibility is his greatest asset, and who all but admitted that Seth Rich leaked the DNC emails (and not some Russian hacker). Additionally, in exchange for a Presidential Pardon, Assange has offered documented evidence to the Trump Administration that the Russians did not hack the election.

Alternative media and Citizen journalists have been covering the Seth Rich story since the DNC IT staffer's murder in July 2016. It was then (and still is) being reported by the MSM Fake News Media as a "botched robbery," despite the fact that Rich was at 4am on his way back from a local bar in a typically safe, quiet DC suburb, where he was shot twice in the back and beaten up without having a single item stolen. Some botched robbery!

> I'm definitely for making an example of a suspected leaker whether or not we have any real basis for it.
> JP WikiLeaks.org/podesta-emails/emailid/45743

This was a clear mafia-style hit. Whoever did it wanted to send a chilling message to any would-be leakers, a threat John Podesta's cited leaked email appears to have substantiated.

Deep State is powerful, but it lacks credibility. The more MSM trots out the belief-beggaring "Russia Collusion" canard, the less credibility Deep State has and the more credible the "Seth Rich leaked to *WikiLeaks*" narrative becomes.

Credit Fox News, and particularly Sean Hannity for being the only MSM outlet to cover the story. Why in response to Hannity's coverage of the Seth Rich story would Deep State via Soros/David Brock's *Media Matters* go to so much trouble to silence Hannity, get advertisers to pull out from his show and get him fired? Answer: because they're desperate to make the story go away! But they failed. Hannity is more popular than ever, and questions about Seth Rich persist:

- DC police have remained silent about Rich. There are no leads in the case. How is that possible?
- Where is the laptop that Investigator Rod Wheeler was told is being stored at either the FBI or DC Police?
- Where is the video footage from the streetlights?
- Where is the video footage from two nearby stores?
- Where is the police bodycam footage?
- Where are the transcripts from those who tended to Rich at the hospital where allegedly Rich was still alive?
- And finally, why is the DNC, the Political Establishment, Deep State, and Deep State's bloggers: the MSM, pulling out all the stops to block, stifle and censor any and all discussion of the Seth Rich case?

For this we know the answer: Seth Rich as leaker rather than Russia as hacker flushes their false narrative completely down the toilet. So what does Deep State do? What they always do when they're caught red-handed. They double down.

Those paying attention and with a modicum of knowledge of Deep State M.O. are capable of putting two and two together to realize that Seth Rich was the leaker, and the DNC and its leadership including the Clintons, the Podestas, James Comey, and Debbie Wasserman Schultz are all serial criminals who are actively engaged in the very long list of crimes they accuse their political enemies of committing.

Once again, the power struggle we see before us between those who wish to do damage control and suppress knowledge of Seth Rich versus Deplorable patriots who want justice, equality under the law and freedom of expression couldn't be more obvious.

The walls are caving in, Globalists. You cannot escape your crimes.

Former head of the DNC, Donna Brazile, dedicated her tell-all book to Seth Rich. Coincidence? Hardly.

#SethRich helped bring down the DNC and Hillary Clinton. The man is a hero and paid the ultimate price. We owe it to him to see that justice is served.

25 Pissed Off about #Parkland!

Jake, I can only take responsibility for what I knew about. I exercised my due diligence. I've given amazing leadership to this agency.

Broward County Sheriff Scott Israel,
CNN Interview with Jake Tapper

The Parkland school shooting hit close to home. I'm a Broward County Florida resident, and to have this tragedy happen less than 30 minutes away from where I live was disturbing. I'm really upset about it. Here are my:

Top 10 Things That Piss Me Off About #Parkland:

#10) **Yet Another Deep State False Flag**: Lone Gunman, Serotonin Uptake Inhibitors, MK-Ultra-esque Mind Control, FBI Stand Down, Police Stand Down, FBI Cover-Up Investigation, MSM Ironclad Narrative. We've all seen this script before. Deep State thinks we're stupid and have the memories of goldfish. The snow isn't sticking nearly as much as it used to, Deep State.

#9) **CNN Town Hall**: Broward County Sheriff Scott Israel, who, much to a cheering, frenzied, hand-picked crowd's approval strutted on stage at the scripted and rehearsed *CNN* anti-gun Town Hall, had the chutzpah to grandstand for votes as he attempted to pass blame for the tragedy and deflect the real responsibility he and his office had for the event on to NRA spokeswoman, Dana Loesch. Loesch needed heavy security to exit the building as many in the crowd were reported to have screamed "Burn Her" as they menacingly surged towards the stage. Way to keep the peace, Sheriff. Way to create a literal witch hunt, *CNN*.

#8) **Using Children As Spokespeople for Gun Control**: Not only does Deep State sacrifice children to wag the news cycle dog in an ultimately futile attempt to distract from all their losing and push their New World Order "Disarm The Public" agenda, it then politicizes and exploits more children by using High School students like Emma Gonzalez (who arrogantly pandered to the audience and "grilled" Dana Loesch at the *CNN* Town Hall) and David Hogg, *CNN* intern and son of an FBI Agent to lead the charge for a completely partisan anti-2nd Amendment crusade against Gun Control. Meanwhile out of a school of thousands, no other kids, many of whom have different political ideas, and some who merely provide contrasting eyewitness testimony that contradicts the mainstream narrative, are allowed to voice their opinions in the Mainstream media. MSM can barely contain itself when it comes to using kids as human shields when there's been a school shooting. This is clearly an attempt to prevent, censor and smear legitimate criticism from alternative media and citizen journalists—but why such silence about rampant pedophilia and human trafficking? This goes beyond the "Double-Standard" argument. It's downright evil. When it serves them, Deep State will kidnap, rape, murder and torture children and then gaslight the public by shamelessly exploiting other children as spokespeople for their anti-family, pro-pedophile agenda. Disgusting!

#7) **The Promise Program**: Turns out that as long as Dade and Broward counties meet their arrest quotas by not exceeding a certain number of arrests of school-age criminals, according to this Obama-era program, these South Florida counties receive millions in state and federal grant money. As a result of this boondoggle, while the total number of arrests are down, overall crime and gang violence by young adults has skyrocketed, and much of that grant money is winding up in the pockets of corrupt politicians. This program could help explain why the Sheriff's office might be more inclined to do nothing about kids like Cruz, stand down during mass shootings, and cover up crimes in general. These are the one who are supposed to be safeguarding our communities but are actually making them far more dangerous in order to line their own pockets and fulfill political ambitions. Sick!

#6) **Broward County Sheriff Department Stand Down**: While the Coral Springs Police Department bravely entered the schoolyard during the event, according to numerous reports (thanks in part to Q Anon posts), at least four Broward County Sheriff Department deputies took up positions behind their cars outside the school while the shooting was going on. Cowardice or an ordered Stand Down? All indications are it was the latter. Sheriff Israel appears to be more than willing to throw his subordinates under the bus if it can deflect responsibility from him. Shameful and unacceptable!

#5) **Sheriff Israel's 23+ visits to Nikolas Cruz's Home**: Scott Israel admits to having visited Cruz's home twenty-three times! Not only is this infuriating, it's extremely suspect. Once again, Sheriff Israel offers no apology for this gross negligence of duty (he prefers to blame "The Killer" and the NRA) and if the event was in fact a False Flag, which everything about it and its False Flag cookie cutter script screams it was, there needs to be a serious independent investigation into Sheriff Israel and his office's possible participation and collaboration with Deep State in perpetrating this tragedy.

#4) **Sheriff Israel's support for CAIR**: Many US False Flag shootings involve Muslim Extremists: 9/11, Oklahoma City, San Bernadino, Fort Hood, Pulse Nightclub, Fort Lauderdale Airport, and Las Vegas. Sheriff Israel has strong ties to the local branch of the Council of Arab-Islamic Relations (CAIR), who many call for to be designated as a Domestic Terrorist organization. Not only that, Deputy Nezar Hamze is a prominent member of the Broward County Sheriff's Department. Hamze moonlights as CAIR's Regional Operations Director. So when we start receiving reports of multiple shooters, testimony from a teacher where the shooter he saw in Building 12 was not identifiable because he was wearing a mask, these are strong indications of possible participation by Islamic Terrorists. Not buying it?

Well, Hamze has conducted active shooter training drills at a Florida mosque, is a vocal supporter of Hamas, and also covered for his cousin, Abdelaziz Bilal Hamze after a brutal "Hit and Run" where a woman was struck and dragged by a minivan for miles that scattered her body parts, a crime from which cousin Abdelaziz attempted to flee the country from. Deputy Hamze later defended his cousin by saying he "may have been a little threatened" by anti-Islamic sentiment, and the Deputy has gone on record dismissing the threat of Islamic terrorism. My guess is that if a proper, independent investigation (and not by a corrupted FBI) is done on Parkland, the likelihood of Islamic terrorist involvement is high.

#3) **FBI's apology for not acting on Cruz's "I'm Going To Be the Next School Shooter" Youtube Video**: When the FBI admits to having known all about Cruz but did nothing to prevent the tragedy, this is a clear red flag to me not just of gross negligence but of participation. The FBI has been rocked by scandal in the past year, and most recently by all the credible claims coming from the recently released Nunes Memo. They desperately needed to inject a new narrative into the news cycle. It worked for a couple of weeks, but with daily leaks coming from credible military intelligence sources like Q Anon, the strategy appears to have been short-sighted.

In the past, when control at the top in the White House was airtight, coverup was much easier and leaks far fewer. Since the advent of the Trump administration, covering up false flags has not only become much tougher, it's also much riskier, as Sheriff Israel quickly found out. Recent events have shown that corrupt FBI leadership (not the many patriotic Rank and File members) care more about protecting the Clintons than protecting children, and they had way too much to gain by implementing a False Flag that at the very least merits serious investigation.

#2) Sheriff Israel Is A Big-Time Clinton Supporter: In a district led by ultra-corrupt Congresswoman Debbie Wasserman-Schultz and an admitted Hillary Clinton supporting Sheriff Israel with his Far Left, Pro-Muslim, Pro-Gun Control, Anti-Second Amendment politics, these are all clear indications that Israel is way too partisan to be an objective player when it comes to fulfilling his local law enforcement duties.

Israel's despicable grandstanding at the *CNN* Town Hall and his total lack of contrition or admission of responsibility has not only not played well in Peoria, it has infuriated huge numbers of local Broward County residents. Israel counted on pre-2016 politics to be able to cover his tracks, but we're in a different ball game now, and all indications are that Israel will as a result of this political paradigm shift be forced to pay a heavy price for his leading role in this tragedy.

#1) RINO Governor Rick Scott's Anti-2A Age Limit Bill: Problem-Reaction-Solution is right out of the New World Order playbook. The fact that it only took a few weeks to get major Gun Control legislation passed in Florida—legislation that changes the age limit to purchase firearms from 18 to 21—and includes confiscation by the State of weapons already legally purchased, speaks volumes to me about how the Florida State Government was just waiting for a tragedy (Problem) to whip the public up into a frenzy by complicit Deep State PR Agency Mainstream media (Reaction) in order to achieve the desired goal of disarming lawful, 2nd Amendment-protected gun owners (Solution).

RINO Republicans, in cahoots with liberal Democrats are alive and well in Florida. The NRA is rightly suing Florida for violating the 2nd Amendment of the Constitution. In the end, I expect that Florida, a very pro-Gun state, will express their displeasure with this legislation at the polls, and Cuckservative Governor Scott will sooner than later find himself regretting his push for this bit of spineless legislation.

Thanks to an increasingly vigilant Deplorable public, President Trump, patriots like Q Anon and those who spread his message, Deep State can no longer have its False Flag cake and eat it too. There are now serious consequences. Doubt it? Stay tuned!

26 Hey Deep State! Who *You* Gonna Call?

If there's something strange
in your neighborhood
Who ya gonna call?
GHOSTBUSTERS
If there's something weird
and it don't look good
Who ya gonna call?
GHOSTBUSTERS
I ain't afraid of no ghosts
I ain't afraid of no ghosts

    Ray Parker, *Ghostbusters* lyrics

```
On Thu, Oct 8, 2015 at 9:26 AM, Tamera Luzzatto
<tluzzatto@pewtrusts.org>> wrote:
```

We plan to heat the pool, so a swim is a possibility. Bonnie will be Uber Service to transport Ruby, Emerson, and Maeve Luzzatto (11, 9, and almost 7) so you'll have some further entertainment, and they will be in that pool for sure. I am ccing Trudy to repeat the invite, and sending pining wishes-you-could-come to Rima, John P, and Laurie & Chris. Con amore, Mrs. Farmer L

From:* Trudy Vincent [mailto:tavincent57@gmail.com]>
Sent:* Thursday, October 08, 2015 11:45 AM>
To:* Tamera Luzzatto>
Cc:* Jon Haber-work; Bonnie Levin-work; Liz Savage; Katherine Klein;> John Gomperts; podesta.mary@gmail.com; Luke Albee; Beth Donovan; Tom> Rosenstiel-personal; Marcus, Ruth (Ruth.Marcus@washpost.com); Jon> Leibowitz-work; Rima Sirota; John Podesta; David Leiter; Laurie> Rubiner-work; Chris Spanos>
Subject:*
Re: Farmers L Update and Welcome Mat

we're in, thanks for the invite.

WikiLeaks.org/podesta-emails/emailid/49435

Deep State is in crisis. It needs false flags to remind the public that it remains relevant. The glue however that keeps Deep State and the Political Establishment together is pedophilia. Unfortunately, unlike in the film *Ghostbusters*, there are no equivalent spookbusters that Deplorables can just phone up and get the problem resolved. It's a lot more delicate and involved than that.

Nations are not monolithic entities. Each has its visible government and its Shadow Government/Deep State. Deep State is committed to Globalism and the New World Order (NWO), and it exists in every nation state, doing everything it can to populate the visible government— whether it be through fear, blackmail, bribery or other tactics—with pliable politicians amenable to the Globalist agenda. Few dare risk ruin by stepping out of line. Fear of exposure keeps them obedient.

When for example dealing with the United States, one always has to ask the question: "Am I dealing with the State or the Deep State?" Same goes for Israel, France, Japan, the UK, Russia, etc. This is a global phenomenon being played out on national stages worldwide.

Right now, if you're dealing with Trump, you're dealing with the State, not the Deep State. I also believe this to be true of Vladimir Putin, who represents the Russian State and not its Deep State. They have not been bought off. They're their own men. Is it mere coincidence that these two world leaders are by far the most vilified worldwide?

While since the turn of the century Putin has earned his Nationalist stripes by resolutely fighting against Globalism, he cannot do it alone. He needs the cooperation of the most powerful nation-state in the world, the United States, led by the people's President, Donald Trump. Together they have a shot at bringing down Globalism, but if kept apart by Deep State, the odds of defeating the Globalists are greatly reduced if not downright impossible.

Deep State ensures that it positions its people at the top of every key institution of both the public sector (government) and private sector (transnational corporations). On a national level, the multinational Deep State combine is primarily a cooperation between the highest levels of Finance, Intelligence Agencies, Media and Military. On an international level, facilitated by world organizations such as the UN, IMF, Word Bank, Bank of International Settlements (BIS) *et al*, each nation's Deep State shares information and largely works in tandem to achieve New World Order objectives.

This system of control has been extremely successful for decades (if not centuries), but what's held it all together, pedophilia, is actually its Achilles heel.

Pedophilia works very well via blackmail as an internal policing mechanism, since all participants are mortally afraid of exposure and as such police themselves. However, what the Globalist transnational Deep State cannot deal with is massive exposure of its pedophilia practices in the public domain, since pedophilia is universally condemned by citizens of the West (but not in the Islamic East) as the most vile crime known to man. It is simply intolerable to the public.

Therefore, news of its pervasiveness in government must at all costs be kept secret. For should pedophilia crimes be revealed, the fact that the practice is so widespread in each of the Globalist Deep States worldwide, exposure and subsequent indictments have the potential to bring the entire Globalist system down. This is why there's been such a huge push in the Globalist Mainstream media outlets and even throughout the public education system to try to normalize pedophilia and downplay its central role in Sharia Law. I'll specifically address the overlapping of interests between Sharia and Deep State in the next chapter.

While public awareness of Deep State pedophilia practices (which includes human trafficking, child murder and organ harvesting) are one thing, enforcement against its perpetrators is another. Unless citizens have the full backing and leadership of national patriots at the highest levels of government, *i.e.* The White House, the Kremlin *et al*, Deep State can rest easily on the "Who ya gonna call?" defense. Deep State counts on the State and its constituents' inability to bring it to justice. With President Trump's passage of his Executive Order that punishes "serious human rights abuses" and "corruption," the quasi-Martial Law ushered in by this totally necessary Executive Order provides the necessary legal tools to not only indict but these criminals successfully prosecute these criminals via Military Tribunal as "Enemy Combatants." This is why Guantanamo Bay has remained open for business.

While rogue elements of CIA, Mossad and MI6 appear to be spear-heading the NWO project, they are aided and abetted by rogue elements within those agencies and institutions of numerous other Globalist-hijacked agencies and their complicit media outlets throughout the world. To be clear, the CIA is not the US Government; Mossad is not the Israeli government, and MI6 is not the British government. The specific mission of those rogue elements is not to defend their nations but to subvert their own governments.

The Putin Revolution of the past 15 years and the current Trump presidency with its commitment to Drain The Swamp is critical to the preservation of the values of the West. For too long our governments in the West have been undermined, subverted and hijacked by the Globalist Deep State intent upon leeching as much of our vital energy as it could. Meanwhile patriots at every level of government and in every government institution have not only been intimidated into submission and gagged by their corrupted superiors, they've also been prevented from even entering into public service! All too often, if you're not marked as a pedophile and therefore easily controlled, entry into the government is blocked. This is a major part of Trump's personnel problem.

The Putin /Trump Revolutions are ongoing counter-coups by the world's two most powerful nation-states and their patriotic majorities, as we battle together tooth-and-nail against Deep State leaders and its minions.

You know Deep State is panicking when it has its lackeys like John "New World Order under enormous strain" McCain openly shilling for the NWO by name! Even after his brain cancer diagnosis, McCain has not backed off an inch from his war against Trump. Be that as it may, all indications are that Steele Dossier scandal-ridden McCain will be retiring from the government before year's end. I for one (but likely for many) will not miss him.

Meanwhile, without even attempting to hide the fact that he's leading 30,000+ trained operatives in his Organizing for Action (OFA) group with the clear and obvious aim of subverting the Trump administration, former President Obama unabashedly leads a literal Shadow Government compound a mere two miles from the White House.

As Alex Jones is fond of saying, "you cannot make this up!"

As a few-in-number, minority power, Deep State can't afford to expose itself as it's now doing. By doing so, it's a sure sign of desperation and a strong indication that we're at the climax or end game of the civil war. The end of the NWO project is only a matter of time, but the struggle is happening right now. Participation of patriots is necessary *right now*.

Remember, over and over again, day after the day, the patriotic citizens of every country in the world are mercilessly pounded (overtly and covertly) by two primary stories propagated by the Deep State's Media wing:

- Russia and the United States must never cooperate
- Pedogate/Pizzagate is Fake News.

Has the Deep State not then shown us our clear path to victory?

To defeat Deep State, four things need to happen:

- Across-the-board cooperation between patriotic Russia and patriotic United States
- Continued, unrelenting exposure of Pedogate/Pizzagate as Real News
- Drain The Swamp by arresting, indicting and prosecuting Deep State pedophiles.
- Create independent pedophilia watchdog agencies at every level of government worldwide: Federal, State, County and City to help ensure that the problem is never allowed to spread again.

Human Trafficking arrests (10,000+) in the US have reached unprecedented levels under the Trump administration. The noose is tightening but the Mainstream media refuses to cover it. Why? Because MSM is and always has been complicit in the cover-up.

For now, our team consists of Deplorables (and other concerned citizens) + Citizen Journalists + Trump + Putin + brave Congressmen like Devin Nunes, Matt Gaetz, Jim Jordan, Steve Scalise and a handful of others in Washington who refuse to succumb to Deep State intimidation and blackmail.

Some Deep State perps will be looking to flip and make deals to save their own necks. This is a positive development. Those who get too close put their lives on the line. We have our work cut out for us, but I firmly believe we're up to the challenge.

Deep State can no longer hide behind the veil of secrecy, and the line of defense extends no further. There's no one left for it to call for aid. It is exposed, isolated and alone.

27 Radical Islamic Terrorism: an Explosive Distraction from the Moderate Threat

Extreme Vetting Question #1: *How do you feel about dogs?*

Mac Balzac

While Radical Islamic Jihadists grab the headlines, growing numbers of non-Jihadi, "moderate" Sharia practitioners pose the real threat to the West. What extreme vetting really means is vetting for Sharia practitioners.

If you have any doubt about the devastating effect of Sharia, just look at what's been happening in Europe. There the threat is clearly not the occasional act of terror, but the devastating social and cultural impact upon the Christian national majority. Left unchecked by the cultural Marxist Left, Sharia operates as a parallel, shadow government and shadow law to the constitutional, democratic Law of the Land.

Increasingly devoid of sovereignty with its forced-open borders, Europe is facing its most dire crisis since WW II. It's become abundantly clear that the unelected bureaucrats in the EU have sold their countries out to the New World Order (NWO). What we see today is an unholy alliance between EU neo-Marxism and Sharia Islam. Meanwhile, the Globalist leadership, *aka* The multinational, transnational Deep State, with the direct aid of the Gulf and Turkish Deep States, have for decades been seeding the West not so much with actual Jihadists but with its run-of-the-mill, culturally and politically incompatible Sharia Islam practitioners.

Although vehemently denied, clearly there is a difference between the public and private face of Islam in the West. Often upon investigation, even seemingly moderate Islamic mosques have been revealed to be promoting Sharia amongst their adherents. Those who support but don't necessarily practice Sharia are waiting patiently to openly declare their full adherence to it once they have Muslim leadership in place and their population has become large enough to make their removal logistically problematic. Unless we can verify that a mosque and its devotees are truly moderate and reformist, they represent an imminent threat to the host nation. To pretend otherwise is simply delusional, although the Political Establishment does everything it can to discourage its citizens from perceiving that reality by smearing them as Islamophobes, Xenophobes and Bigots.

The Migrant Crisis in Europe has turned a once tourist-friendly region on its head. Greece, Italy, Spain, the UK, Germany, France, Sweden, Belgium and Holland have all been hit hard. Burying one's head in the sand is no longer an option. The countries least affected: Poland, Hungary and the Czech Republic have all risked heavy sanctions from the EU for keeping their borders closed, but clearly that's essential. The whole EU project has been one big Trojan Horse.

Wars were fought for centuries in Europe to hold off the Muslim invaders with their brutal, intolerant ideology and slave trade. Thomas Jefferson's concern about the "Barbary Pirates" was a direct reference to the Islamic threat. Failure to recognize this situation for the war it truly is will likely prove fatal. Not only must the short-term effects of the Migrant Crisis be dealt with, but a long-term strategy is vital to staving off the inevitable demographic time bomb that will make Muslims too numerous to contain in the not-so-distant future. The UK, France and Germany already appear to have gone past the demographic tipping point.

Decades of cultural Marxist education and Mainstream media brainwashing have done a number on the native populations of Europe, leaving them terribly vulnerable to such an attack from Sharia. Europeans have been sold down the river by their governments and largely been cowed into submission. There (and to a lesser but not insubstantial extent in the US), by design, MSM refuses to identify the problem as Sharia-Islamic, as it goes against the terms of the Multicultural social contract. What began a few decades ago with arresting people for espousing revisionist views of the Holocaust has now morphed into an all-out attack on Free Speech throughout Europe. While the ideologically bankrupt Left spreads its legs for the New World Order, and Sharia continues to demonstrate its obvious incompatibility with the values of Western Civilization, tough decisions on the strategy moving forward must be made.

First of all, we must call a spade a spade. Sharia Islam is an existential threat. It can take the form of terrorist acts, but even more alarming is the way it spreads from one generation to the next and radicalizes itself as the Muslim population grows. That must be nipped in the bud.

I've always been a firm believer in the idea that if what

you're doing doesn't hurt anyone, it's not a problem, but if you are hurting others, all bets are off. While Sharia does hurt many of its own adherents, particularly women, children, homosexuals, and anyone who violates its codes, if Muslims wish to practice it in their own countries, I won't begrudge them for it. I do hope they will reform it themselves, but that's up to them. Meanwhile, it's truly nothing personal when I strongly advise banning any and all Sharia Islam practitioners not only from coming into Europe and the United States, but also recommend the peaceful deportation of Western-based Sharia residents who do not wish to discontinue the practice.

That may sound harsh to some, but we're not out to win a Social Justice popularity contest. Our entire Western Civilization is at stake here. We can no longer afford the luxury of rationalizing too lenient a policy against clearly incompatible Sharia practitioners by saying that the internment of Japanese-Americans during WW II was cruel and unfair. It certainly was insofar as it really was based on racism rather than ideology, whereas with Sharia practitioners, we're dealing with ideology not race.

With Populism and anti-Globalist sentiment surging in varying degrees throughout the Western hemisphere, the UK, US, and to a lesser but not insignificant extent in France, Germany and The Netherlands (despite not winning the Presidential elections in those countries) and throughout much of Europe, there is for the first time in decades reasons for cautious optimism.

But make no mistake; this is war! It's war against the Globalists, and war against one of its primary weapons: Sharia-Islam.

So what can be done here in the United States? Here are a few suggestions that specifically apply to the United States, but can also be implemented in Europe:

— Tourist Visas for Sharia-Islamists can be issued, but no permanent residency. It's simply too risky. Western governments' primary obligation is to protect its own citizens first, and unfortunately Sharia Islam has proven itself countless times throughout history to be a danger to everything the West stands for.

— At the local level but based on nationwide strategic policy, there must be a greater commitment to infiltrating the mosques (which essentially function as military barracks) so that national governments can know which mosques are truly reformist, and which ones are Trojan Horses. Undercover spies and journalists—particularly those patriots of Muslim cultural heritage—will be essential to this effort.

— Non-Governmental Organizations (NGOs) and organizations based in the West that finance and support Sharia law in the West need to be banned and expelled, and if terrorist acts are financed by or conducted through these same organizations they are subject to being outlawed as terrorist organizations.

— Even with the Travel Ban approval by the US Supreme Court (after much nonsensical obstruction by the 9th Circuit Court and hysterical squeals from the Left), don't hesitate to expand the ban to include other nations who threaten our security with incompatible beliefs. Though it's not politically correct to say it, the majority of those countries are Muslim. Sorry, they just are.

— Declare the Council on American-Islamic Relations (CAIR) and the Muslim Brotherhood as Domestic Terrorist organizations. This is surprisingly difficult, as these groups are well-financed and maintain a strong presence both institutionally as well as throughout Deep State.

— Continue the practice of Extreme Vetting.

— Get the very sensible RAISE Act passed in Congress, since it supports an economic merit-based system for Green Card applicants which should serve as another layer of protection against bringing in incompatible Muslims.

— End Chain Migration.

— Build The Wall.

— At the geopolitical level, maintain a thorough understanding of the unique conditions of each of the major players in the Middle East: Saudi Arabia, Iran, Turkey and Israel and craft pragmatic foreign policy strategies for each that reward good behavior and punish bad behavior. The spreading of Saudi Wahabist ideology coupled with Turkey's bellicose pro-Islamic policies and large overseas populations in Europe have actually played a much bigger role in creating the Migrant Crisis than Iran.

Meanwhile the Israeli Deep State's "Greater Israel" policy has helped destabilize the region by encouraging the spread of radical Islam (in order to weaken national unity and make its neighbors less militarily strong) at the expense of moderates and Christians. The War in Syria has been Exhibit A in illustrating the devastating consequences for the Middle East and the World when all this bad behavior from these States (much of it stemming from their Deep States) is encouraged rather than thwarted. From a diplomatic perspective, economic carrots and sticks should prove most useful.

If after successfully passing through the necessary rigorous vetting process, self-sufficient, hard-working Muslim people from other nations demonstrate a sincere wish to embrace our values, love our people, love our land, and respect our laws and customs, we will welcome them with open arms. But if that is not possible for those who have a long history of bloodshed, conquest and enslavement, clearly see us as Infidels, wish us harm and harbor a long-term goal to erect a new Caliphate within our lands, those enemies will be bitterly opposed and sent back from whence they came.

We like our dogs here.

Ruff.

28 Head for the Turn Around

Paid the cost to be the boss
I'm a bad mutha, heh
I'm a bad mutha
Head for the Turn Around
Head for the Turn Around
Told you so!
　　　　　James Brown, *The Boss*

The United States seeks to impose tangible and significant consequences on those who commit serious human rights abuse or engage in corruption, as well as to protect the financial system of the United States from abuse by these same persons. I therefore determine that serious human rights abuse and corruption around the world constitute an unusual and extraordinary threat to the national security, foreign policy, and economy of the United States, and I hereby declare a national emergency to deal with that threat.

President Donald J. Trump
Executive Order, December 20, 2017

I grew up playing chess, so I really appreciated Q Anon's reference to the famous 1918 match between Frank Marshall and Jose Capablanca, where Marshall, after years of preparing for the match against his nemesis, formulated a brilliant attack using the black pieces, something that is very unusual and difficult to pull off since white always move first, and chess masters know

> My enemies thought I had been vanquished, that I would go into hiding in the hills of Dartmoor with my dick between my legs like some weak ass pussy faggot. All they've done is piss me off.
> Milo, *Dangerous*

how to maintain that advantage throughout the match. The problem was that once Marshall's brilliant opening attack did not succeed, he left himself vulnerable to Capablanca's inevitable and what would prove to be devastating counterattack.

Today, in the Spring of 2018, the Globalists are Marshall and the Nationalists are Capablanca. Deep State is Marshall and Trump & The Deplorables are Capablanca. The Globalists threw their full Deep State financial, media, Big Tech and Intelligence Community weight into attacking Donald Trump and his supporters throughout his first year in office but failed and left themselves vulnerable to counterattack.

They tried to rig an election and still couldn't win. Instead they left themselves open to investigation of the massive election fraud they themselves committed.

They tried and failed to overturn the results of that election via recount. This also exposed their own election fraud.

They tried illegally spying on the President and unmasking a wide net of his associates and failed. Instead, by committing serious crimes against the government, perjury, treason and seditious charges are set to be handed out against all the perpetrators up to the highest levels that include Hillary Clinton and Barack Obama.

They tried and failed to convince the American Public that Trump is a racist. Instead they exposed their own racialist hypocrisy and double standards by only supporting minorities when they conform to liberal narratives.

They tried and failed with the #MeToo movement to frame

Trump as a Sexual Harasser. Instead they exposed their own secret Congressional Slush fund used to cover up their many crimes of pedophilia and sexual harassment.

They tried and failed to sell the idea that Trump's crazy. Instead, they look crazy by hysterically insisting that Trump is crazy.

They tried and failed with the Mueller Special Counsel to show that Trump colluded with Russia. Instead, they exposed their own criminal collusion with Deep State Russian and Ukrainian actors.

They're trying to get rid of the 2nd Amendment and will fail at this too, because most Americans recognize it's essential to their protection against crime and tyranny.

They try with false flags to justify their relevance and only expose how irrelevant and dangerous to the public they actually are.

America is woke, Deep State, and we're fighting back. Hard.

Parkland was a terrible tragedy, but the Democrats and their Globalist backers are, predictably, politicizing it in order to try to disarm the population. Want to know what disarming the public brings you? It brings you Muslim invasions that you can't speak out about it without getting fined or imprisoned. Merkel's Germany is Exhibit A. Is that what we want in America? Disarm the public and they no longer have any leverage against tyrannical regimes.

That's why we can't play defense against Deep State.

When given the opportunity to counterattack, just as Capablanca was able to do against Marshall, we too must fight with every ounce of our strength and pool together all resources against an unrelenting enemy who won't hesitate to frame and murder us and our families. They lie and they spin and they attack without shame or mercy. Love thy enemy but give it no quarter. Kill it not physically but politically.

The Nunes Memo was a perfect example of an opening counterattack move that was without US historical precedent. For once, the Right made the Left play defense in a sustained way. Just as *WikiLeaks*' drip-drip-drip approach during the 2016 election was so effective at undermining Hillary by exposing the DNC's rigging of the primaries against Bernie Sanders, while also clearly demonstrating the Left's disgusting predilection for pedophilia as evidence by the Podesta emails, the hubris and the *chutzpah* of the Obama/Hillary/DNC/FBI/DOJ/NSA "Insurance Policy" with its abjectly false and salacious claims against Trump has been exposed for the treason it is.

Truth is on the Deplorable side. The rank and file of the Police, Military and Intelligence Agencies are all on our side. These insurance policy-type antics would have worked in the past, because there was not enough political will or actual power to fight back against the corrupt leadership of these Deep State-run institutions. But now we have like-minded individuals in Deep State willing to bravely take a stand. We have Deep State leaders like FBI Director of Counter Intelligence Bill Priestap flipping on the FBI and fired director James Comey. How did this happen? Comey perjured himself on multiple occasions in front of Congress and unwisely tried to throw Priestap under the bus with his testimony.

That's why having that beach head with Trump in the White House has made all the difference. The rank and file throughout the government, honest patriots from both the Right and the Left are fighting back against corruption. Against the Fake News Media. Against the Clinton Crime Syndicate. Against Hollywood. If Jeff Sessions does his job, it's Game Over, baby.

Speaking of Hollywood, Mrs B and I recently watched Chris Rock's new comedy special on *Netflix*. The first 10 minutes were appalling race divisive unfunny garbage: "I wanna see a world where an equal number of white kids are shot, where white mothers cry on TV," while the rest of the show was non-political and funny. What's going on here? Well, let's just say it's pretty clear that if you're Chris Rock and you want the big bucks that come with having your comedy special headline on Netflix, you better have at least part of your act address their Globalist, Identity Politics, race-baiting talking points. That's why the show feels so schizoid, like two different shows in one.

I live in a pretty racially diverse area of South Florida. I go to the gym and I'd say it's probably 60-70% black. We all get along. There are no racial incidents. Ever! It's all media hype. There is no "Alt Right," (*aka* Neo-Nazis) or Ku Klux Klan that I can see. Instead, it's a tag-teaming mainstream media and the Democratic Party who regularly fan the flames of racism, especially anti-White racism in this country. But it isn't real. In the overwhelming number of cases, it's fake, fabricated. and manufactured to divide us among ourselves.

The Globalists try to put a nice Liberal smiley-face mask over their genocidal New World Order agenda. It's not working. We're fighting back, but we have a long way to go.

We need to push the envelope on expanding our own media reach. Though they have some warriors like Sean Hannity, Judge Pirro and Tucker Carlson, overall Fox is way too defensive and centrist to carry the Deplorable message. Essentially they're MSM gatekeepers.

We need at least 5 more *Infowars*-style, Deplorable agenda-driven shows to compete against the Fake News Media. We need our own comedy shows. Comedians like Mark Dice and Gavin McInnes who are also brilliant and articulate are so much funnier than anyone you see on *Saturday Night Live*. We should go head-to-head against *SNL* with our own late night comedy shows and our own late night talk shows. This is all part of the counterattack, which isn't just political, it's cultural. Andrew Breitbart, may God rest his soul, was absolutely right when he said, "Politics is downstream from culture."

It's tough to fund these communications operations. We have to start small and grow organically because TV stations won't carry us. Radio somewhat, but TV no. Twitter, Youtube and Facebook are heavily politicized and are not reliable platforms that can be counted upon in the long term. As James O'Keefe has shown, these social media behemoths engage in widespread censorship of Deplorables. Expect to be shadow-banned, and even, like Roger Stone and Milo, kicked off these platforms. The bad news for the Globalists is that banning people from Social Media only makes that person's brand stronger and their message more credible. It's called the Streisand Effect.

Trump's recent issuance of the Executive Order to fight serious human rights abuses and corruption was a major step that has gone almost completely uncovered in the Mainstream media, but as soon as it went into effect, the CEO of Google, Eric Schmidt, resigned. As a form of Martial Law, which admittedly is a drastic but necessary step in draining the swamp, this opens up the ability of the government to prosecute offenders as enemy combatants and war criminals in military tribunals where they can't lean on their appointed, corrupt liberal judges to exonerate them. Goodbye penthouse, hello Guantanamo.

When Hillary lost the election, the Globalists were faced with a stark choice: admit defeat, cut their losses, make a deal and live to fight another day; *or* fight to the death. They chose the latter. They are Marshall. We are Capablanca, and we are about to roll their asses up.

29 Basic Bitch to Deplorable Patriot

On occasion, it can be good to go against your instincts and habits just to shake things up, to see life from another perspective, or simply to take a chance. Repetition can put you to sleep. Sometimes you have to look for opportunities to respond differently and break the mold.

Donald Trump
Trump 101: The Way to Success

9/11 Red Pill

911 was a wake-up call that not only popped my self-absorbed bubble but shattered the illusion of the benefits of Globalization. Distracted by mindless entertainment and unnecessary bling, my generation had been asleep at the switch while America was losing its way. Though I remained fairly apathetic towards politics, from that moment on, I began to reassess the foundation of my political understanding. I wasn't exactly sure what happened that fateful morning, but after the MSM and politicians in Washington told us their version of the events, I came away certain that the Alice-in-Wonderland fantasy the public was being told wasn't even close to the truth.

Because the lines have been so clearly drawn, we Deplorables can easily determine according to actions taken who is playing for which side. For those who don't choose to view politics through the Globalist/Nationalist lens, the actions taken by politicians occur largely along party lines without any overarching agenda. For the walking dead, newspapers only exist to sell papers. These folks don't deny that Mainstream media does spread a little propaganda, but that's far too messy a subject to incorporate into their world view, so they choose to ignore it. I don't.

Same goes for corruption. Since it's often difficult or impossible to prove corruption, many choose to ignore it as a driving factor behind a politician, media head or CEO's course of action. Too messy. Too difficult to prove. But just because we don't always have proof (though sometimes proof does exist) it doesn't mean we're incapable of recognizing patterns of corruption and criminality. We Deplorables have been blessed with discernment, and we have common sense.

Others, as smart as they may be, have a blind spot when it comes to the criminal mindset. I'm essentially a good person, but I'm not naïve. I don't just take people at their word or look only at the surface of events. I dig as deep as I possibly can, triangulate multiple sources of information, scrupulously observe actions and make provisional determinations accordingly.

That people work together to achieve common goals is an obvious core element of human interaction. But to suggest that Globalists conspire to move humanity and the planet one step closer to a New World Order has long been considered crazy. But is it really?

Experiencing eight years of Globalist George W followed by eight years of Globalist Barry (and then re-examining with a fresh set of eyes eight years of the Crooked Clintons of the 1990s) sealed the deal for me in terms of understanding that our country had been—by design—sold into slavery and royally screwed.

Caveat Emptor

I'm a Trump Cheerleader *up to a point*. If I had to give President Trump a grade for his efforts thus far, I'd give him an A-. Why the minus?

While President Trump is right to criticize the obstructionist Democrats, a party that's certainly lost its way and has little to offer the American Public, the Republicans are hardly much better. What we have in this country is a 2-Party Duopoly. Trump's genuine populism is an anomaly.

For this reason, apart from the occassional political rally, failure to more meaningfully and frequently interact and connect with the Deplorable Base is a major problem moving forward. Trump cannot forget that without The Movement, he won't stay in power long. The Movement trumps The Man.

The President already has great difficulty passing legislation in a GOP House and Senate. Imagine what will happen when the Democrats have a majority in Congress? How will Trump be able to govern then?

We Deplorables are a patient bunch, but our patience is not unlimited. We need leadership that can leverage all the new media tools at its disposal and doesn't just concern itself with the Legacy media. Leadership that will speak up and stand up to domestic terrorism from the Left. Leadership must vocally make its case to the American people to get its own people into key administration positions.

While I feel that President Trump has the chops to convert most or all of these minuses into plusses, it's time to start actually doing it.

What more effective way is there to stick his thumb in the eye of the Fake News Media than giving vocal support to the Alternative media and Citizen journalists who actually have his back?

Why not expose to the public just how impossible it's been to get Trump Supporters into the Administration? The President needs those people for his own protection!

And for all the President's genius on Twitter and his experience as a Reality TV Star, how is it that after more than 15 months into his administration there's been nothing creative, imaginative or effective in terms of communication strategy beyond his own Twitter account?! To me, that's alarming.

Trump dishonors The Base when he fails to stand up for their 1st Amendment rights. Trump also fails to protect the Base's back when there are numerous physical attacks from Antifa and no accompanying commentary from him or his administration. But if Alex Baldwin happens to do a mean Trump skit on *SNL*, POTUS is all over that with multiple tweets!

Trump not only needs to match the level of engagement he had with the Base during the campaign, he needs to increase it tenfold if he wishes to keep it energized and capable of seeing him through the rest of his term. Trump's margin against a motivated Left is too thin to lose any hard-fought support, such as with those who voted twice for Obama and only once for Trump.

Let's not forget:
- How many, out of the 47,000 applications made through MakeAmericaGreatAgain.gov, were hired by the Trump Administration? Zero.
- How many times has Trump tweeted about Alec Baldwin making fun of him on *SNL?* Many times. But how many times has Trump tweeted about his own supporters getting attacked and beaten for wearing a MAGA hat? Zero.
- How many times has Trump tweeted or spoken out about Antifa violence against his supporters? Only once in passing in the midst of Charlottesville, but never since.
- How many times has Trump sat down for an interview with his most ardent supporters in the media? With loyal supporters like Bill Mitchell or Alex Jones?

There's still *lots* of work to be done here, folks.

But bitching time's up. Upward, onward and all aboard...

...The Trump Train. Chooooo-Choooo!

When I first heard Donald Trump on the air, I was only mildly impressed. He came across as a brash yet colorful and humorous guest on Howard Stern's radio show. Trump seemed particularly fond of sharing with the audience his appreciation of beautiful women—which no doubt was the bawdy Stern's main reason for having him on his show. Nevertheless, when he began doing his TV show, "The Apprentice" and then "Celebrity Apprentice," I somewhat sheepishly found myself becoming a fan. Although I realized it was television, Trump impressed me with his business savvy, sharp intelligence, keen eye for the vagaries of human psychology and behavior, as well as his sober judgment with which I only rarely found myself disagreeing. Additionally, the man gave every indication that he really cared about each participant on the show. He wasn't just some cold businessman. Though he was tough when he had to be, he was clearly an empathetic person, a trait many assume is common but is actually quite rare.

As a father myself, I can also appreciate that it takes a special man to raise such great, remarkably grounded kids as Don Jr, Ivanka, Eric and Barron—especially when those kids grow up super-rich and are subjected to all the temptations and social baggage that comes along with that.

If an American icon like Trump could run a successful multinational business while simultaneously helping raise such an admirable family, why couldn't this man succeed as President? Was it really such a leap? As long as he was serious about running – and initially we weren't sure he was—here was a man I could actually get behind.

Incidentally, once Donald Trump's two terms in office have been completed, I'll be first in line to join the Donald Trump Jr (or Matt Gaetz or Devin Nunes) campaign.

My initial thoughts on the election were fairly limited, but once it became clear that Trump was really going to run and wasn't just doing it for publicity as some in the media (like Howard Stern) were claiming, I began to sit up and take notice. Listening back then to Trump speak about his Nationalist/Populist agenda was both welcome and surprising. Who knew this was what Trump was really all about? Wow! At that point it dawned on me that the country was in for something it hadn't seen in a long time —a genuine patriot who was neither a puppet nor out to screw the American people.

Getting the opportunity to challenge two arch-Globalist candidates like then GOP Establishment favorite Jeb Bush in the primaries, and then if Trump was able to get through Bush and all the bevy of other candidates in the Primaries (which was still considered very much a long shot), and then Hillary Clinton in the General Election, it became clear that the Globalist agenda would be exposed in unprecedented ways. So even if Trump were to lose, just by running, I could see that he was poised to create a major stir.

The fact that Trump—despite Jeb's overwhelming advantage in fundraising—was able to swat the silver spoon of privilege and legacy out of his mouth was nothing short of astonishing. I wasn't quite sure yet what my role in this American drama would be, but my soul was beginning to sing!

The tipping point for me, and I expect for many others, came on September 10th, 2016, when at a New York City fundraiser, Hillary Clinton referred to Trump supporters as a "Basket of Deplorables" and awoke the sleeping giant. Thanks, Hillary!

Hillary's outrageously disparaging accusations made it clear like never before exactly what we know we're not: racists sexists, homophobes, xenophobes and Islamophobes; and exactly who we are: American Patriots who are sick to death of Political Correctness, cultural Marxism, Identity Politics, Sharia Law, a lack of border protection, the rights of illegal immigrants counting more than legal immigrants' and Citizens' rights, and a corrupt, anti-Free Speech, entitled, Globalist Plutocracy out of touch with working and middle class Americans hell-bent on monopolizing everything and everyone they could lay their grubby little traitorous palms on.

As mentioned throughout this book, while President Trump is the *de facto* head of the Deplorable Movement, this Movement can and must endure beyond Trump (One of its greatest strengths is that it has no leaders!). This is not a criticism of our president, it's just that winning the Culture War and MAGA does not rest on the shoulders of any one man or woman.

As of the time of this writing, I strongly approve of about 90-95% of what Trump's done. Let's face it; that's outstanding. With Obama and Bush, that ratio would at best be reversed, and if Hillary "Madam President" Clinton had won, it would probably be even less.

En fin, let's keep on runnin' our meme machines full blast. They're deadly to The System, good clean fun, and great for the soul.

Yup. Shoulda killed me last year.

DJ T

The @POTUS

Black Unemployment?

The Lowest

Not to brag

But it's lower than Obama had

Rap deplorable

Hot wife's adorable

Gotta beautiful wall

And it's totally affordable

Rhymes are sage

Never fail to persuade

Dems just jealous

Welcome to The Golden Age

rap by Mac Balzac

www.ingramcontent.com/pod-product-compliance
Lightning Source LLC
Chambersburg PA
CBHW060746050426
42449CB00008B/1309